Wrestling for your Life

Wrestling
for your
Life

Darrell McDowell

Front Cover – Mark Jahad, 2005 NCHSAA-Division AAAA State Champion 189lb weight class. Wrestled for Jerry Winterton at Cary High School, near Raleigh, North Carolina. Photo provided by David Maney II, CHS Sports Information Director.

ISBN: 1-59571-114-7
Library of Congress Control Number: 2006921653

Word Association Publishers
205 5th Avenue
Tarentum, PA 15084
www.wordassociation.com

Table of Contents

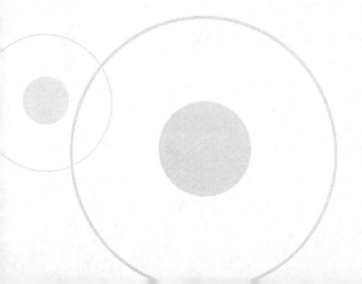

Foreword

Summer was over and as a ten year old I began school in Lana Jones' fourth grade class at Etowah Elementary School in rural Western North Carolina. The smell of oiled floors in the corner room of the old brick building where my mother had graduated from high school was fresh and clean. Like in the years that preceded that one, I was very happy to be back in the comfort of all that I knew about life and education. Everything was going along fine during the first few days in my new class and then we were asked to do an assignment that included writing a two-page paper on what we had done during the summer. I quickly and happily began writing about playing with my brother, fishing in the creek down by the barn and riding my pony "Trigger" in the pasture in front of our one bedroom house that we rented for twenty-five dollars a month. It was pleasant to think about and easy to write because it was real and it was true.

All went well until several of the other students began to read the reports about their experiences during the summer. When they began to talk about their spectacular visits to Myrtle Beach, Disney and Gatlinburg, I began to get a little nervous about the content I had to offer to the enrichment of the class. I remember monitoring my heart rate with my hand as it felt like it would come out of my chest as we neared my time to speak. At no time in my short life prior to that event, did I recall such a strong feeling of insecurity about who I was and where I stood in the eyes and the expectations of my peers and my teacher.

When the time came for me to walk to the front of the room, the rustling of the papers and the creaking of the wood floors seemed to echo the sound of my thumping heart. The longer I read what I had written the more the content of my experiences seemed to pale in comparison to the other students in the room. All of the self-criticism in the world seemed to engulf me at that one time as I stood in the middle of a stark awareness of my shortcomings that I had never experienced before. The fact that I was overweight, poor and ashamed had never been quite as clear as it was on that day. It was at that point that my view of my inadequacies melted down what was left of my hopes for finishing the reading of my paper. I began to cry and I ran out of the room. My wonderful red headed teacher followed me into the hallway. She got me some water and did not require me to return to the front of the room.

As children do, I recovered from the experience and I moved on with my life, but some of the questions about who I was, and what I had to offer were left unanswered for several years following that emotional day in Ms. Jones' class. It would not be until I was introduced to the opportunities and experiences that I found in the sport of wrestling that I would learn to face my fears and my circumstances. The lessons I've learned as a result of my participation in this game have not only taught me about finding courage, but it has given me a level of peace and security that allows me to embrace the experiences and the deficits that I have had with confidence, pride and even thankfulness.

As I continue with my extended education and I work toward obtaining the course-work needed to finish a doctoral degree in Educational Leadership from Western

Carolina University, I often reflect on that day in my fourth grade class, and I am quick to recognize that what I have learned on the wrestling mat has been the most defining element in my persistence to find success in all areas of my life. The text you are about to read is loaded with people who can attest to the advantages that can be found in the sport of wrestling.

Thomas Ferguson – Thomas earned a fourth place finish as a sophomore competitor in the AAAA Division of the NCHSAA State Tournament for Cary High School in 2005. He is coached by Jerry Winterton.

Photo provided by David Maney II, CHS Sports Information Director

Left to right – Alvin McDowell, Center-Darrell McDowell and on the right is my little brother Dale McDowell- Alvin and his five siblings are my first and third cousins. His daddy was James or "Coot" as they call him. Coot and Grady (my dad) were brothers. Sylvene (my mother) and Alvin's mom Juanita were first cousins. The McDowell brothers were from Crab Creek, nestled at the foot of Pinnacle Mountain, and my mother was from Big Willow where I would eventually grow up fishing for trout from the banks of Willow Creek.

1

Wrestling: The Big Picture

Not too long after the incident in Mrs. Jones fourth grade classroom a man came by the house and asked if my brother and I could play little league baseball. I actually thought for a minute that it could happen since my daddy had played a little cow pasture baseball in his day. But that chance was over as soon as the man drove out of the yard. Grady (Daddy) came up very tough. He was a pretty rough cat. He had to quit school in the tenth grade and his enthusiasm for athletics was not very high. My mother had been a good basketball player in her day at Etowah High School. But that was when everyone lived close enough to the building to walk the two miles home from practice if they needed to.

I had been going to Rugby Junior High School for two years when I made a final attempt to ask to play football. Up to this point the only result I had gotten from asking to play football was the back of his hand on the side of my head for asking again after he had already told me to shut up about it. One thing he did do was spend a lot of time in the woods with my brother and me. He loved to hunt and fish and fortunately for me I had a cousin who lived in

Hendersonville, who had the same fever for the outdoors that my dad had. His name was John Ballard, he was my age, and he loved to spend time out in the country at our house on the weekends. He was better off financially than us and he would visit our Big Willow home very often. We were close friends and he went to Rugby Junior High School along with my brother and me. But he played football. He came in from the city and I went about nine miles out to the school on a bus everyday. He was the kind of guy who would eat raw fish eggs as we were scaling and cutting the heads off the bream we caught out off the farm ponds in Henderson County. I think that feat was kind of impressive to my daddy for some reason. Anyway, at some point between the squirrel hunting, coon hunting and fishing my daddy finally caved in on letting me play football, that is, if I could find a way to get back and forth to practice, because we only had one car. Brian Ritter was a boy I went to Beulah Baptist Church with and he was willing to help me with the two miles that separated our houses. I still remember the shock on my parents faces when I had to tell them that practice would be everyday of the week.

Well I went ahead and played that year. My weight was still on the heavy side when I began the season, but by the end of the football season I had lost some of my baby fat. On a Saturday after football season I returned the favor with John Ballard and went into Hendersonville to visit him at his house. We were walking down the street when Coach Tony Varnadore pulled his step-side Chevrolet pickup truck over on the side of the road and asked if he could give us a ride home. He was one of our football coaches so we agreed to get in. He then told us he was getting ready to start the first wrestling team in the history of Rugby Junior High School.

John was a basketball player so that left me with the only question to answer. I knew at that very moment that I had to try to find way to do the sport. I did not have the $10.00 for shoes and it was a struggle to negotiate with my parents for a chance to compete. Fortunately for me the same boy who was able to give me a ride in football had also decided to wrestle. So I was able to find a way to make it work. I owe a great debt to Brian and the Ritter family. This turn of events eventually led to a chance for me to go to college. And on the day John Ballard graduated from high school he drove his truck to the great outdoors of Montana and he has rarely been back. The grass always seemed to look greener for both us on the other side of the fence. And it was.

This book was written in an effort to capture the passion and the enthusiasm among the athletes, coaches and fans of amateur wrestling. This sport has the potential to change behavior, inspire personal development, and set the pace for a productive life and a fulfilling future. There are few activities that remain in today's society that push the body and extend the mind to an extreme point of self-realization and personal growth as this unique and ancient sport of wrestling.

The United States is saturated with enormous arenas for football, basketball and baseball games. Unfortunately amateur wrestling is often over-shadowed by these "big three" sports, whose games are heavily attended and whose rules are understood.

The continuous exposure to these popular events in the public domain helps to ensure a participation rate that recreates itself, and is handed down from parent to child with a cycle of value and appreciation that has reinforced their growth and their stability.

Varsity football game at East Henderson High. Coach Brett Chappell vs. Hendersonville High School. Coach B.J. Laughter at Justus Field, Fall 2005

Unfortunately, there are few resources available for parents and coaches to turn to when they want to familiarize themselves with the details, the rules, the history, and the excitement of amateur wrestling. Obstacles that often limit the growth of amateur wrestling include the lack of an established cultural tradition, coupled with a shortage of educated and experienced coaches. There is often a lack of common knowledge about the sport among parents, administrators, and community members. This deficit can sometimes create an atmosphere of low expectations and lack of consideration with regard to the performance standards that are set for coaches and wrestlers in some schools.

This secondary status is often reinforced by a lack of attention to the needs of the sport by school administrations and is further complicated by weak hiring practices when it comes to searching for a competent wrestling coach. This unfortunate dynamic can diminish the level of enthusiasm for the sport and lower the eventual rate of funding and success for the program.

But the most blatant reality that limits wholesale participation in the sport is the mental, physical, and emotionally grueling nature of the contests. The day-to-day intensive levels of preparation and practice necessary for success requires a depth of commitment that tends to separate, sort and sometimes eliminate many potential wrestlers. The requirements and expectations that have to become a necessary part of the process in this game can, for some athletes, become a participation-threatening consequence, especially if they are already struggling with their level of dedication, or if they are questioning their personal belief in themselves.

2

A Level Field of Play

The time I spent on the football field in a uniform, being told that I could do anything I wanted to do and be anything I wanted to be hit home with me. The recognition, the sense of team and the exhilaration of the physical contact had eased many of the doubts that I once had about my capacity to contribute. I was on fire with the possibilities that might exist in the athletic arena. When I put on the singlet, helmet, uniform, or headgear it was all the same to me in the ninth grade. I was just like everyone else and with a chance to prove that I might even be better than some at this newfound place of equity and opportunity. And the individual nature of the competition that could be found on the mat even further intrigued my sense of ambition about engaging in the sport of wrestling.

○○○

Personal sacrifice in this sport can be tremendous. Yet, amateur wrestling offers many opportunities that are often overlooked by many mainstream student/athletes that choose to participate in the revenue sports. Although the challenges that are inherent in the sport of wrestling are clearly great, and can be both physically and mentally demanding, the individual potential for becoming successful can offer a fair and equitable process for making your own way as a champion.

Unlike some sports that can often richly reward athletes for possessing the benefit of God-given individual traits such as size, height, weight, speed and gracefulness, the sport of wrestling ignores some of these natural advantages. This sport is categorized and organized by weight divisions rather than allowing the unbalanced discrepancies that occur among athletes in some sports. In fact, even some athletes that have significant physical handicaps can often find ways to be creative enough to be competitive in wrestling.

Many inspired athletes and motivated leaders find avenues of contribution in this sport when they might have been eliminated from any chance to participate in other athletic events. Wrestling embraces individual differences, imagination, and technical expertise. This sport often rewards the athlete that is most attentive to developing an intensive work ethic, and to those who have a persistent belief in their own abilities. This sport tends to segregate participation and success by levels of heart and character without much regard for the physical blessings that are bestowed upon the genetically advantaged.

Many of the skills and the character attributes that are molded in wrestling are easily transferable to meeting the demands and challenges that we face each day in our personal trials. The complications or confrontations that we are often exposed to in educational, occupational, legal, and interpersonal scenarios will test some of the same areas of our integrity, composure, and sportsmanship that are needed for participating in this sport.

The degree to which an individual has to reach down to muster up the ambition, confidence and intestinal fortitude that it takes to be successful on the mat can become an excellent resource for ensuring personal success in business and in life.

One extremely successful example of the benefits of amateur wrestling began at Southern Alamance High School when Coach Wally Burke had the opportunity to get Bobby Lloyd Bynum to come out for his wrestling team in the 1970's. This young man was not born with a "silver spoon" in his mouth. And he, like me, had very few of advantages that are available to a more privileged segment of society. In fact, many might have questioned his level of personal potential until he found the sport of wrestling. Bobby became so successful in the game that he became Coach Burke's first all american wrestler.

Coach Bynum spent the next eighteen years working alongside Coach Burke. He assisted as a coach with the program at Southern Alamance, and continued with his efforts during the years of enormous success that he and Coach Burke enjoyed at TW Andrews in High Point, North Carolina. During that same period of time, Coach Bynum was also focused on pursuing a vision for success in the business world.

Coach Burke gives great credit to the contribution that Coach Bynum has made to the sport of wrestling, and he quickly illustrates the kind of man that Bobby Lloyd Bynum has turned out to be since those first days that he began wrestling in high school. Coach Burke is also quick to tell you about the outstanding business that Coach Bynum has built for himself in the Winston Salem/Greensboro area. He began his trade by loading trucks and driving buses, and now he owns "Bynum Tour Buses." And, when Hurricane Katrina hit New Orleans, he was one of the first companies to volunteer his line of buses for the services that were needed at the Gulf Coast.

Bobby Lloyd Bynum – Outstanding Assistant Coach at Southern Alamance and High Point Andrews High Schools.

Both Coach Burke and Coach Bynum are glowing products of the amateur wrestling fraternity that exists in the sports world. They preach discipline, character, competition and sportsmanship and then they practice it. Their kids believe what they say because they see a consistent demonstration of professional posture and a sincere level of integrity. And it has been apparent in the success of their programs.

Coach Bynum still works with the young people in the Greensboro/Winston Salem area when he can make the time away from his day job. He can be found contributing with practice at TW Andrews, Glenn, High Point Central and Mt. Tabor High Schools.

High Point Andrews High School at the NCHSAA Dual State Champion Match, Coaches Wally Burke and Bobby Lloyd Bynum.

The work ethic and self-confidence that can be gained in this sport often elevate the former wrestlers into prosperous employees and entrepreneurs. The ambition that is learned in the sport can sometimes help to invigorate the overall climate of an organization and inspire the participation of other members on their staffs as these former wrestlers lead and model their motivated contribution on the job.

The Starting Line-up

*A*ll the enthusiasm in the world could not help sidestep what awaited me for the first two years of my wrestling career. Although I was a fair athlete, I had never been on a mat before. Neither had most of the other competitors that were in the practice room on that first year team. Coach Varnadore was enthusiastic and demanding in his first job as a head coach. And, I was struggling. I was having great difficulty with the technical aspects of the sport. I wanted to learn. But the details of the game were really foreign to me. I was competitive in wrestle-offs but I seemed to always fall just short of making the starting line-up.

Then toward the end of the season I finally made it into the line-up against Waynesville Middle School out of neighboring Haywood County. I was wrestling in the 145lb. weight class. It felt great to be back in a position to compete again in a real contest like I had been able to do during my first year in football. I remember the boy's last name was Ratcliffe and he didn't look that tough during weigh-ins. But when the whistle blew it became clear that my assessment of his ability was a clear underestimation of his potential. During the third period I ended up on my back.

That was bad enough but then he flopped his body on my head. I couldn't move. I didn't want to get pinned. And, worst of all I couldn't breathe. So in my fourteen year old moment of perceived desperation, I bit him on the stomach. Needless to say he let me up. Not one of my finer moments in the game, but effective. I am certainly not proud of what happened during that first match. But desperate people do desperate things.

With a conference champion in my weight class during my first season as a wrestler at West Henderson High School, I had a similar type season as a sophomore on the varsity team. I did finally beat him at the end of the season and wrestled one varsity match that year. But as a junior and senior I had a very productive experience, finally making it to the semi-finals of the NCHSAA State Championship in 1979 at Parkland High School where I lost in a 5-4 match at the 185lb. weight class.

The sport of wrestling has always had a way of purifying itself. There is often a process of natural selection that occurs in this game that can be more extreme than the procedures that are found in other sports. It is rare to find the same clarity and purity for prescribing starting positions among other athletic teams when compared to the process that is most often used in wrestling. Individual success is dictated by in-house competition and performance contests rather than the coaches' preferences. This process allows little room for the politics or parental persuasion that can, and often does, occur in other sports.

Wrestling parents often have to learn the hard way to accept the realities of their child's performance. And then, they have to learn how to deal with the sometimes-harsh results of their child's level of performance in the very public and visible matches and tournaments. The critical and often emotional accusations that are made about coaches in other sports are far less available to the parents of wrestlers. These athletes are equipped with a level of instruction and then they are released to define their own destiny and to sort through the most effective strategies that will be needed as they are competing on the mat.

Wrestling can be a very high-risk proposition. It takes a great deal of tenacity and courage to put on a singlet and step on to the mat to face an opponent in such an aggressive and personally demanding environment. Sole responsibility for individual success and that of the overall team lies in each participant's efforts to dominate and manipulate the strategy that is being initiated by his opponent. When things go well and victory is achieved, there is a tremendous sense of satisfaction and elation. But when the wrestler falls short of personal and public expectations it often requires an enormous amount of reflection and character.

In wrestling no advantage can be found by blaming another teammate for their mistakes and shortcomings. On the mat, you can't say he missed his block, or she wouldn't throw me the ball. Acceptance of personal responsibility separates wrestling from many other athletic activities and often eliminates potential wrestlers from participating in such an isolated, hard-fought and pressurized experience.

Troy Neal vs. Enka at West Henderson High School. Wrestler Troy coached by Darrell McDowell. Opponent by Jim Whitmer. Troy was a NCHSAA State Place Winner.

Not all individuals are mentally wired to embrace the constant potential for personal humiliation that can accompany defeat in this arena. The weight of all the drama that evolves in the center circle of the wrestling mat often reveals the true stature, posture, and composure of those who engage in this substantial challenge.

4

Leadership and Sportsmanship

*D*uring my senior year at West Henderson I high school we took a wrestling trip to Mitchell High School in Spruce Pine, NC for a dual match. All went well. The final team score was 66-12. I pinned my red-headed opponent in the first period and we were ready to head down the Mountain from the highest point this side of the Mississippi in a matter of just few minutes of competition. But, before we left we stopped at a Hardees's Restaurant in the city of Spruce Pine. That was our first mistake.

I went in with my warm up on and I had big white towel wrapped around my neck, talking a little bit of junk and feeling pretty good about myself. We ate, got back on the bus and began pulling out of the parking lot onto the main road. We hadn't gone a half-mile before a blue light came on behind the bus. An officer got out of the car that made our heavyweight wrestler look like "Tiny Tim." He was huge. When he got to the passenger door of the bus he asked Coach Cliff Wilson, our head coach, to step off the bus. It didn't sound promising. A few minutes later Coach Wilson got back on the bus and said, "Which one of you *called this man a pig during the time we were eating in Hardees?" There was dead silence. No one would confess to this crime. Coach Wilson then looked at me and said, "Darrell, we are not going anywhere until someone talks to him about the problem." It was at this point that I had never felt worse about being elected captain of the wrestling team. I got off the bus and went back to the squad car. He said, "Get you're a_ _ in the car." He then said, "I ought to take you up to the court house right now. I don't know how you treat law enforcement down there in Hendersonville but when you come up here on this mountain you will treat us with respect." I tried to explain that I was acting on behalf of the team as a liaison for the program but I don't think he heard a word that I was attempting to say. I think if I knew then what I know now and could do it over again, I would have said "Then take me to the court house." Probably not, but it sounds exciting to say it.*

The next day the coach found out that one of our sophomore wrestlers had actually had alcohol in his gym bag and he was the one who had been brave enough or dumb enough to call the officer a pig. Needless to say, he was removed from the team and suspended from school. And I was well on my way to a career in leadership. What a way to start.

The potential to develop leadership attributes as a wrestler is endless. Courage, risk taking, discernment, and persistence are just a few of the necessary requirements that are cultivated and refined during the training and conditioning experienced in a successful wrestling program. The lessons learned in wrestling competition provide immediate and long-term consequences that have to be dissected and reconstructed in the mind, and then reproduced effectively with the body in an effort to ensure improvement and success on the mat.

It is rare to find consistent opportunities for our youth that allow for individual performance under extreme conditions, while encouraging a contribution toward the success of other team members. The self examination and reflection that takes place in this athletic arena, that some would characterize as volatile, or at the very least, emotionally and mentally exhausting, can critically define an individual's ability to perform under difficult circumstances in other diverse or conflicting situations in their lives.

This sport requires absolute attention to achieving an individual level of composure and sportsmanship. The physical and personal nature of the game can create a variety of dynamics in practice and in competition that test our expectations for pure and consistent self-control. The game requires a sincere sense of mental and emotional self-discipline.

The adults that attempt to coach wrestling have a tremendous responsibility to share expectations and model behaviors that are consistent with the common requirements for maturity and self-control. The personal attributes of discipline that are required in this sport often reinforce and help substantiate many of the characteristics that will be needed for engaging in future situations in life where teamwork and leadership will be rewarded. Most of the young people who dare to engage in the wrestling arena will be well equipped as they begin to take on the responsibilities in the working world.

5

Coaching Wrestling

Coaching: Practice at the Appalachian State University Summer Wrestling Camp 2005.

I am often asked if I miss coaching. My normal response is "everyday." I have often thought about my packaged answer to that question and that response is probably not really a true statement. What I do miss is playing the game. I miss the physical contact in football and I miss the high level of intensity on the wrestling mat, the adrenalin, the chance to succeed and the sense of well-being that can be attained by defeating your opponent as a competitor in the athletic arena. But being on the edge of the mat and preparing individuals to become successful young people does have its own rewards that can make coaching almost as engaging as participating.

Coaching wrestling is about as close as you can get to participating in an event without actually competing head-to-head as a player. Not all coaches engage in the same level of physical participation during practice that I do. If you coach it that way there is a small margin of physical risk for both you and the athletes on your team. But sparring with and physically instructing your athletes during the practice sessions will enhance their performance. The older you get the more difficult it can be to maintain the high level of physical engagement that you may be able to use during your early years in this business. But it is very important to have someone on your staff that can demonstrate specifically how techniques are to be performed. And it is also better if your athletes can see it done at the pace and the level of intensity that will be needed when it is used in a match.

Coaching wrestling offers an element of comradeship, fellowship and emotional intimacy that is not often found between coaches and athletes in other sports. Much of the connectedness found among the participants in this game is due to the extreme personal highs and lows you have to face in this type of one-on-one competition. This excessive level of adversity and intensity can be very attractive to some people. I happen to love it.

Many of the same expectations that ensure success on the mat for wrestlers are also required as a prerequisite for becoming a successful coach in this sport. Time, energy, persistence, technical expertise, and personal sacrifice will all figure into the formula that is needed for administrating a successful wrestling program.

Providing the essential skills for success in wrestling requires a genuine level of enthusiasm for teaching and improving athletic performance. Unfortunately, it is rare that you are able to find qualified candidates to coach wrestling that are competent in every facet of the game. Some of the necessary requirements that will have to be considered while searching for a strong leader for your school will include a rich understanding of the technical, emotional, psychological, and physical needs of your athletes. And they will need to have communication skills to clarify their expectations in an understandable and effective manner.

Like most other sports, finding success with the technical aspects of wrestling lies in the strong understanding of, and the consistent pursuit of, the fundamentals in the game. The most effective skills are usually well-understood and easily recognized in the elite programs in the country, and they often ultimately determine the difference between victory and defeat in a highly competitive environment.

Many times the problem for coaches in wrestling can be in finding a successful way to clearly articulate effective moves and strategies. Problems can quickly arise for coaches who haven't had the benefit of participating in a sound high school program, club, or university level of competition.

Wrestling offers avenues of creativity for finding a way to win that often exceeds the options found in most other sports. But there are still certain fundamental areas of skill in the game that can be objectively clarified as being either the "right way to do it," or "the wrong way".

No coach ever intends to send a wrestler on the mat unequipped to face the harsh realities that can be delivered by a well-drilled and strategically prepared opponent. It can be a tremendous and heart-breaking burden to be placed in a coaching situation that exceeds one's expected level of performance and expertise, and that can often create an unsafe environment for the participants. Learning how to get into a correct stance or determining how to land on the mat during a throw are crucial ingredients for success and safety. Incompetent coaches may never cover basic survival skills with their limited or lack of previous experience as a wrestler or as a coach.

6

The Confidence Factor

The first year I went back to my alma mater at West Henderson High School as an assistant football coach and the head wrestling coach, I was running the in-school suspension program at the school for students with behavior problems. Before the wrestling season even began I had started recruiting a little bit and there was one particular student that I didn't have to ask to be on the team. About once a week he would come by the mobile home that I used as a classroom down by the parking lot to let me know he was going to be on the team. He was a junior and the first thing he ever said to me was about how great he was going to be that year. He said that he had heard that I knew a little bit about the game and that was all he needed to get him over the hump.

Frankly his physical condition in September made him look like about a forty-year-old. He had long red hair and a beer belly. And he was not really a muscle bound or even athletic looking kid. But, he never missed a beat with his consistent assurance that he was going to set the world on fire that year. His name was Rick Atkinson and I truly thought at the time that he was probably an arrogant little want-a-be wrestler. He had not had great success the year before, but he was adamant about what he was going to do as a wrestler even as I challenged him a little bit about the fact that he had done nothing that I could see that was impressive to that point. The former team had been 3-11 with their victories the year before and had not sent anyone to the NCHSAA State Tournament in the five years before I arrived as the new coach.

Well the season came and the first day Rick looked no different than he had when he had shown up at my classroom. In fact some of the kids, and me too in fun, would sometimes call him "doughboy." But he quickly began to change my mind. He started practice at a weight of about 205lbs. And granted I worked those poor kids extremely hard in an effort to turn the corner with the losing culture that they had become accustomed to at that time in the school's history. But, the big red headed Atkinson kid ate it up. He loved the work and he began to shrink. He quickly began to drill and wrestle, like a mad man. Everything he said to me about being willing to do what ever it took to become a champion, he apparently meant. The problem was that he had to wrestle 195 early in the season and as the year went on his weight began falling toward the 185 pound class and then he was shrinking toward 171. He had lost a number of matches at the heavier weights during the time that he was just beginning to perfect his skill level.

After the conference tournament that first year I arrived at the regional seeding meeting that qualified students for the state tournament with all my kid's records. Rick's record was barely 50/50. By that time late in the season, he was truly a 167 pound athlete. As we began to look at the competition it became clear to me that because of his record, he might not even be seeded in the bracket at 167 or 185 pound weight class. It was at that moment that I made a drastic decision to move him all the way back up to the 195lb. weight class. It was a big gamble. But over the course of the year, I learned to love this kid's level of ambition and his incredible level of self-confidence. He ended up being the 15th seed in a 16 seed regional bracket at the 195lb. weight class, which meant that the next morning he would be facing a kid from Pisgah High School that had a record of 32-2 and weighed almost 25 pounds more than Rick. And to make matters worse the kid from Pisgah was married and had a wife and kid of his own. These were the kind of odds that most people would avoid at all costs. But Rick saw this chance to compete as an opportunity.

I won't tell you that I wasn't concerned about the decision that I had made. But there was a little part of me that had an element of hope simply because I knew that if anybody on our team had a superior belief in his newfound abilities to wrestle it was this cocky little red head. What happened next could not have been scripted with any more energy, passion or disbelief. When Rick entered the mat it was clear that he was in the wrong weight class. The height and weight differences were glaring. But in the third period of the match the superior work and conditioning on Rick's part began to pay off. He pulled the Pisgah kid's shoulders to the mat and pinned the number two seeded 195lb. athlete to move on to next round of the region.

Rick was on fire and I was too. We began a strategy that led him to two more pins at that weight class. And then as fate would have it, we looked around the arena and Rick was *standing on the mat in the finals of the NCHSAA Regional Tournament. He was in a match where he would have to compete with William Hemphill. William was a physical beast who was coached by Rex Wells from Brevard and this was the year that William would eventually finish 2nd in the state and the Brevard team also finished 2nd in the state. When the whistle blew to start the match we knew it would be a difficult task and Rick went on to lose to William in a 12-6 match. But it really didn't matter. Rick was a hero. He proved to everyone in the building, including me, that he had a belief in himself that no one else had. He will never know what he did for the birth of what would go on to be an outstanding West Henderson wrestling program.*

The next week after his regional Cinderella story he competed in State Tournament at Carmichael Auditorium in Chapel Hill where he had to eat a big breakfast to make the 195lb. weight class forcing him to weigh at least 169lb.'s to make the cut-off. He made the weight but he didn't have much success in Chapel Hill in 1987 at that weight. But he finished a very respectable 3rd place in the NCHSAA State Tournament during the next year in 1988 as a senior in the 171lb. weight class where he belonged. The year after that, his little brother Rob won the state championship in 1989. Rick's level of confidence and belief in himself was referred to often and emulated regularly long after he graduated as a West High Falcon.

As wrestlers start to feel that they understand the game and begin to gain confidence in the technical concepts of the sport, a good coach can begin to use this opportunity to start establishing a genuine level of competitive performance.

Clearly, it is one thing to perform a skill on a drilling partner, and another to reproduce that skill's effectiveness in the contest environment. But developing a level of confidence requires a long-term prescription for success, rather than a one-time injection of instruction, or a minimal exposure to a demonstration of even the most effective strategy.

Continuous encouragement, with an enthusiastic expectation of improved levels of performance, will often help stabilize and reassure some of the doubts that can arise with the early failures that will be experienced by newcomers in the live wrestling arena, even in practice.

Individuals that are well-schooled in the fundamentals of the game will normally prevail against the less experienced athletes in the room. At this point many advantages can be gained for the individuals who are struggling by developing a recipe for improvement that combines high expectations and constructive criticism. This approach needs to be contrasted and balanced by the infusion of genuine, and emotionally charged, positive reinforcement. This breakdown and recuperation process, supervised by enthusiastic, skilled, and caring coaches, can pay tremendous dividends that will reinforce the confidence and the progress of individual wrestling performance.

Critical, intensive, and sometimes harsh experiences can be used to develop courage and character traits that transcend the mat environment. Many of these regimented and extensive experiences can have beneficial advantages for your wrestlers that will be used as a resource for making progress in other areas of life. The critical coaching techniques and experiences that may have to be used to secure a genuine and authentic level of self confidence for your athletes in the wrestling game may have to include elements of reasonable levels of physical suffering, labor intensive extremes of endurance, visionary hopefulness, and opportunities for ensuring a chance to experience elements of personal triumph.

State Champion, Derrick Gardner from D.H. Conley High School on the Top Podium. His Coach, Milt Sherman awards him the Gold Medal in the 1989 NCHSAA Tournament Finals.

7

The Physical Attributes

The most significant Christmas gift I ever received I bought for myself in the ninth grade when I was wrestling at Rugby Junior School. I had saved about twenty dollars and my brother had been given a similar amount. My parents took us down to a discount store on 7th Avenue in Hendersonville, NC to let us get whatever we could afford. I remember that Dale (my brother) who is a year younger than me purchased a cassette tape player and I had other interests. I had just finished football, was losing weight, and had been exposed to a little bit of weightlifting at wrestling practice. That was all that I needed for me to fall in love with what I thought lifting weights might do for me. I had already discovered the magazines that included photos of Arnold Schwarzenegger, Franco Colombu, Sergio Olivia and Frank Zane with their massive physiques.

As I scanned through the possibilities at the discount store I noticed a set of 110 lb. plastic weights sitting in the corner with a small bar and a handbook that included a picture of some big guy on the front cover. My quest was over. We put them in the old car and took them to the house. My grandfather had a woodshop and he took a 2X10 board and made me a homemade bench press that is still at my parent's house to this day.

When I was a Junior at West Henderson High School my offensive line coach and head wrestling coach, Cliff Wilson, allowed me to borrow his fifty and twenty-five pound iron plates. There were many times that I remember rolling the bar down my chest to get it off of me when I would work out at home alone. I would not advise using that particular approach. But, I often had no spotter. You do what you have to when you are as motivated about the weights as I was back in the day. I kept the coach's weights until I graduated. I was eventually able to bench press over four hundred pounds before leaving high school.

I later even got into the bodybuilding scene in college winning the Mr. Mountaineer Contest at Appalachian State University in 1982. And I finished 4th place in the 1983 Mr. Atlantic USA Contest that was held in Spartanburg SC. I eventually got out of the physique contests. I never participated with any kind of steroid use. That fact would have made it very difficult for me to compete at the upper levels of the bodybuilding competitions. I was a Health and PE major at ASU and then I became a teacher/coach in my career. I was convinced about staying away from the dangers of any kind of drug use. Illegal steroid use just doesn't fit well with what I believe is wonderful about weightlifting.

Pumping iron changed my life for the better in many ways. It helped me in football, wrestling, bodybuilding and overall health. But it also gave me the confidence and the discipline to pursue many academic and other challenges in life.

The advantages created by improving the physical attributes of the body can also affect the confidence factor. Although wrestling and weightlifting are not necessarily always positively co-related, it is rare that you find an individual who is successful in wrestling that does not believe that there are legitimate advantages in developing a consistent weight-room routine, especially in the off-season. One of the most significant advantages for lifting weights and improving levels of strength and endurance begins with the transformation of the body, and transfers as a powerful advantage to the mind of the wrestler.

Cameron McDowell training in the weight room at East Henderson High. Coached by Barry Cannon at East Henderson High School.

There is a component of confidence that is often acquired by the athlete as he/she begins to develop physical advantages. The physical transformation usually enhances their belief, at least at a mental and emotional level, that they have worked hard enough to become a stronger and more effective competitor. Their mental perception of an increased level of strength and a renewed sense of confidence in their potential to perform is usually enhanced with the benefits that are gained as a result of their hard work and improved physical prowess.

Most individuals not only gain confidence, but they also begin to believe that they truly deserve to win. In many cases this improved attitude helps ensure a greater resistance to any negative thoughts of conceding to an opponent in difficult situations on the mat. This element of physical and mental fortitude factors back into the importance of supporting and frequently encouraging athletes to strive for an essential belief in their own abilities. This bridge of pride and confidence has to be crossed at some point in the competitive journey as the athlete processes toward championship wrestling status.

Efforts to ensure a high level of physical strength and personal success on the wrestling mat can often enhance other areas of personal growth and development. The physical changes that occur as young men mature toward adulthood, when supplemented by a disciplined approach toward lifting weights and improving physical stature, can lead to greater personal goals and expectations in other areas of their lives.

The sense of confidence about the obvious changes in the new and improved version of these young adults that can occur because of gains made in the weight room may push them to enthusiastically participate in activities that they might have previously by-passed. Whether it is in another athletic event, a new social activity, or a new confidence to deal with some previous fear that they might have had, they are often better equipped to find the courage to participate and extend themselves with a greater sense of security and ambition. A newfound stature, posture and sense of self-respect can open many doors on and off the mat.

Darrell McDowell in 1982. "Mr. Mountaineer" winner at Appalachian State University's Annual Body Building Contest.

8

Work Ethic

*D*uring my third season at West Henderson High School *it was early in the conference schedule when we arrived at North Buncombe High School for a dual meet with Coach Herb Singerman's Black Hawks. Herb's squad was a young team that was making progress and at that point on our schedule we were undefeated in both duals and tournaments for the year. As the match proceeded we did not perform with the sharpness that we had grown accustomed to seeing when we stepped on the mat to compete. When the heavyweight match was over that night the score was West Henderson 48, North Buncombe 24, but it was sickening. We looked almost as bad winning as we had looked during the first year I took over the program. We celebrated what we could from the win, but I was visibly upset about the overall performance.*

We got on the bus and drove through Asheville to get back to the high school. I had warned some of the parents before we left North Buncombe that we might be late that night. I had asked the kids in the locker room to leave their singlets on until we got back to West. When we walked in the gym I turned on one big light in the center of the floor, over the mat and I told them to change into their running shoes. That was about all that I had to say to them on that evening. We turned the music up loud, ran three miles, drilled for thirty minutes and wrestled for thirty more and we went home.

We won the rest of our regular season matches on the schedule and went on to have two state champions and the team finished third in the state tournament that year behind the runner-ups from D.H. Conley and the champions at High Point Andrews. The work ethic we had was probably the single most important factor in any of the successes we enjoyed. Kids want to work. But sometimes they have to be reminded of the rewards and encouraged about the depth and the breadth of the task.

Many of the attributes that support and ensure success as a wrestling athlete are learned behaviors, reinforced by a consistent and regimented focus on detail, and a grinding level of intensity. A strong work ethic provides the discipline and the perseverance that will be needed to endure the intensive process included in improving performance. Many students learn the value of the work and begin to enjoy the benefits of their efforts as they begin to see advancements in their abilities to perform on the mat. Typically students need to see consistent results in order to stay focused on the task at hand while participating in any area of their life.

Wrestling often provides tangible and concrete evidence of how a genuine focus on detail, drill and repetition produce successful results. The enthusiasm and attention generated as visible evidence of progress begins to occur, and the level of intensity begins to climb, can often start a chain of reaction in the practice room that becomes a contagious affair. In fact, on the great teams, this almost euphoric level of pride and confidence in the process, almost certainly has to occur if team goals are going to be met.

The work ethic and the consistent routine for providing opportunities for advancing their skills often becomes a "synergetic experience." The sum of all of the individual's performances in the practice room begins to exceed the benefits that are contributed by each one individually. When this dynamic happens it can become an exciting and productive time in the practice room.

As evidenced at high school state tournaments all over the country, and in families that are immersed in the sport of wrestling, where you find one state champion, you will often find two, three, or even more outstanding wrestlers. These committed associates are often found near the same weight class, engaging physically and competitively in the same practice room, or in the same family environment, where they gain from each other's examples of success.

The rewards and accomplishments of individuals who find exceptional success in wrestling often begin to bleed over into the visions and ambitions of those around them. There examples of performance and confidence begin to influence the people who are close enough to the success to be well informed about the benefits of making such a committed decision in the sport. The examples they set among their peers and family members often act as catalysts for the birth and the generation of entire programs and traditions.

The process and the journey that leads wrestlers to this place of exceptional performance cannot be easily understood and appreciated without having been exposed to a series of obstacles, challenges, and rewarding revelations. The appreciation and the attainment of this type of work ethic and conviction most often occurs in an environment dictated by an expectation of extreme individual risk-taking and a high level of personal and physical sacrifice to be successful in this game.

The Ellenbergers

One very impressive family of athletes that resides in the Carolinas who have committed themselves to the requirements and the rewards of amateur wrestling are the Ellenberger's. Tim and Tom Ellenberger are twin brothers from the first generation of athletes that will be discussed, each of whom had outstanding careers at East Carolina University. These brothers wrestled for John Welborn, who was a former Appalachian State University coach and wrestling standout.

Tim Ellenberger was a three time Southern Conference champion and Tom was a three-time runner-up as an outstanding competitor for the exceptionally successful Pirate team during the late 1960's and in 1970. During their senior year Tim won the "Most Outstanding Athlete Award" at ECU. And at that time both Tom and Tim won North Carolina Collegiate Championships. Tom was voted "Most Outstanding Wrestler" for that particular tournament when it was a part of the former collegiate structure in the Southeast.

Both Tim and Tom went on to have impressive high school coaching careers. Tim coached in North Carolina for a time at Brevard High School before leaving the game to begin a career in school administration in Transylvania County.

Tim continued to officiate wrestling in Western North Carolina for many years after his coaching days. Tom went to South Carolina where he has had continuous coaching success in the Palmetto State. During his time as the head coach at Rock Hill High School he directed their outstanding program to their first of many South Carolina State Championships at the school.

Tim initially had two children named Timmy and Mark. Each of these young men became State Champions in North Carolina during the late 1980's and early 1990's. Timmy was a two-time State Champion and he earned the MVP Award at the state tournament during his sophomore year victory. Both of these young men now coach at the high school level in North Carolina. Mark works at his alma mater at Brevard High School in Transylvania County. Timmy wrestled two years at the University of North Carolina at Chapel Hill before being plagued by a shoulder injury and he now helps out as assistant coach at Ragsdale High School in Guilford County, near Greensboro, North Carolina.

As time went on, two more brothers were born into the family of Tim Ellenberger. Mark Ellenberger coached the two younger brothers Joe and Tom, who also became student/athletes at Brevard High School. They were also successful in the North Carolina High School State Tournament in the early 2000's. Each were two-time place winners, and each of these two younger brothers won over 100 matches for Brevard as they made heavy contributions to the Blue Devil's team success, leading their High School to an NCHSAA Individual Tournament State Championship during the 2003 season. Their older brother Mark, along with Coach Vernon Bryson from Brevard, also shared in the process of forging the team victory.

Coach Mark Ellenberger, with brothers Joe and Tom Ellenberger at the NCHSAA State Championship Tournament in 2003.

During the same year that Joe and Tom were a part of the NCHSAA Individual State Tournament Championship in 2003 that was won by Brevard, the oldest brother Timmy was an important part of the coaching staff at Ragsdale, where his team won the Dual Team State Championship Tournament. Following their high school careers, both Joe and Tom have now become students at the Citadel in Charleston, South Carolina, and both will likely continue in wrestling careers for the Bulldogs. This dedicated network of family success clearly highlights a common work ethic, an enormous passion for the sport, and a culture of well-understood expectations among these ambitious family members.

All four Ellenberger brothers with NCHSAA State Championship rings.
Left to right: Joe, Timmy, Tom and Mark.

Tim Ellenberger and Family at the Citadel in Charleston, South
Carolina.

As verified in the picture below, it appears that this extraordinary family has an incredible history in the sport of wrestling, and the future looks bright for a new generation of athletes in the sport. Tanner is Mark's son. He is the one with the medal around his neck. He and some of the younger Ellenbergers are already competing and winning matches at the youth level in the sport.

Tanner Ellenberger with uncles Tom and Joe.

Creating a Culture
of Success

West Henderson wrestlers with 10 Finalists in the thirteen weight-classes in the AAA Conference Tournament at North Buncombe High School in 1988. Coached by Darrell McDowell. Visible in picture from left to right: Tyler Brock, Robb Atkinson, Brandon Curtee, Troy Neoh, Todd Murphy, Taylor Sullivan, Derek Irvin, Rick Atkinson, and Keith Arbogast.

*W*hen West Henderson decided to upgrade the quality of their cafeteria, it was a time when our program had been successful for a number of years. The day that the administration sent an artist down to the In-School

Suspension classroom to find out what I wanted painted on the wall for a wrestling mural alongside football and basketball, I knew we had begun to change the culture of the school with the impact we had made as an organization. There were only a limited number of murals that went up in the building. And for the most part, they were dominated by the "big three" sports. But the significance of our contribution could not be ignored. It was really only a symbolic gesture of our importance. But it gave our kids a sense of pride in the fact that they were wrestlers.

As wrestlers begin to mature and learn to embrace the high expectations needed to endure and find success in their sport, they begin to not only accept the work and the sacrifice, but they become prideful about their participation. In fact, if you ever become fortunate enough to be a part of experiencing this type of transformation on your team, be careful about how your leading wrestlers are promoting your process, and the degree to which they begin to create legacies and legends about the hard work you are doing.

Having a large number of dominating superstars who are telling stories about surviving the practice room can actually discourage potential wrestling candidates from joining your program. They may decide it would be too hard for them to join your team even before they come out and give themselves a shot a being successful.

A great way to avoid this concern about surviving the potential demands of your program lies in making sure that coaches provide supplemental opportunities for the young members of the team. These inexperienced students need to participate in a number of Junior Varsity Tournaments and preliminary matches that will ensure their chances of obtaining some level of success with what they have learned in the practice room.

You will need to use some wisdom as you prescribe your early practice sessions to avoid the urge to immediately "feed the young ones" to your physical and technical beasts that normally reign over the mat at the varsity level. At least wait until your rookies gain enough experience to have a chance of battling your elite kids before you do too much live inter-squad competition, especially if there are clear disadvantages with the physical or technical discrepancies in the skill level of your JV group and your Varsity kids. Give them a chance in the first few days of training to leave the practice room with some element of self-respect left in tact.

There will be plenty of opportunity for ratcheting up the competitive level as the young ones begin to embed themselves into the program. Gauge their performance as you go, and challenge their level of improvement as needed. Plan to integrate them with the Varsity during the later part of the season.

Do not create a hole in your program for the future by squeezing them out of the practice room before they are able to get a tight grip on the fundamentals. If you are doing your job, these new and talented individuals will gain the advantages they need to allow for their survival in the powerful structure of your program, especially if they truly want to become a legitimate opponent in the sport of wrestling. With this having been said, many will still fall by the wayside, due to the extreme nature of what will have to be done to ensure the success of the program.

Wrestling teams that are finding success with their programs normally create a culture in their schools, and in their communities, that begins to replicate itself much like the "big three" sports have been able to do over the years. Oddly and ironically enough, the same degree of difficulty and sacrifice that tend to eliminate a number of potential athletes from participating in wrestling seem to also provide the backbone for the culture that evolves out of the sport.

Wrestlers tend to take great pride in the fact not everyone can, or is willing to, endure the toughest elements of this "business." As each individual commits to immersing himself in the sport, pride begins to overshadow any of the obstacles that might have once hindered their will to participate. Most of the initial growth related to the birth of successful programs begins with a determined coach who has a dream of developing a championship team.

If you are considering this proposition, be prepared to make an exceptional commitment to forfeiting extreme blocks of time and effort to the needs of cultivating your program-to-be. You will regularly sacrifice significant parcels of personal family life to ensure the wrestling team's ultimate success. If you are committed to a marriage or another relationship, you need to discuss your intentions with these people as fully as possible before you enter into this challenging agreement. This is not to say that it can't be done. In fact, it can become a rewarding experience for everyone. But in truth, you will need the support and a committed understanding about the depth of this proposition that you are considering by all who are associated with your vision for the program.

As the coach begins to cultivate the participation, growth, and the number of wins needed to turn the heads of students, parents and the media, and as the personal and team recognition begins to headline the organization, you will find that almost "everybody" begins to want to become associated with your program. Everybody loves a winner. Problems finding assistant coaches, statisticians and camera people often begin to dissipate as the win column begins to grow. Opportunities for providing food for team meals, buying uniforms, educating parents, and providing transportation become abundant when success becomes evident. At this point, you will begin obtain the power and authority to start creating a strong wrestling culture.

Coach Darrell McDowell, West Henderson High School, holding the Trophy after winning the Annual Crest Tournament in Cleveland County, North Carolina.

A strong coach can establish expectations for all stakeholders by modeling the posture and the vision for the program through his actions and his leadership. The birth of an outstanding wrestling team can be delivered out of this enduring vision. To initiate and sustain a successful program, you will need to show a willingness to do some hard work, attend various speaking engagements, and negotiate opportunities that accentuate the growth of your program.

As you begin to establish success, fan support will begin to increase. And over the years, you are likely to accumulate a base of parents that are willing to contribute to your program, even after their child has graduated and gone on to work. And a small number of wrestlers will move on to competition at the university level. This achievement will often help develop a more enthusiastic interest in your program and enhance the culture of wrestling in your school, and on your team.

The return of the "old heads" (former successful wrestlers) will illustrate a further advantage to the participation in your wrestling program. They can provide some unique opportunities for obtaining new and fresh elements of technique and an increased understanding of the importance of the game. Some will be able to demonstrate cutting edge skills from the college practice room. In wrestling, most college level kids will want to revisit the old "stomping grounds". Most are normally willing to come back around Thanksgiving, Christmas and spring break to share exciting new details about how they are fairing at the university level.

Kyle Kuykendall, in down position, Southern Conference Champion at Appalachian State University (Coach-Paul Mance) and NC State Champion (Coach-Darrell McDowell.)

Don't be afraid to let them explain some of the drills and conditioning methods that they have learned as a participant on a team at the college level. If you have done your job while they were in high school, you can feel secure about what they are attempting to share. Make them feel welcome. They will still have a sense of investment and loyalty to what you have shared with them from their past ventures in your program. And, your current high school kids may gain some motivation and ambition about what may be within their own reach at the college level.

10

The Fraternal Order

I was working in my office at East Henderson as Assistant Principal when my secretary said I had a phone call from Abner Bullins. It had been about 10 years since I had seen him. He was the first kid I had ever coached at Madison Mayodan High School that had qualified for the NCHSAA State Championships. He was a great kid. He worked very hard on the weights and he was an outstanding football player. He lived with his mother in Madison and he had a heart of gold. He was almost too nice for his own good. He was a kind young man and he was a 195 lb. physical specimen. The most difficult thing about coaching Abner was getting him to sustain his sometimes brutal approach to the game of wrestling. Although he had his moments when it could be scary to be on the same mat with him when he truly expressed his physical ability.

Abner had to deal with other issues as he pursued his efforts to wrestle. His cousin Jonathan Bullins had just won a NCHSAA state championship as a heavyweight at Madison/Mayodan the year before I became the head coach there. Jonathan had become somewhat of a hometown hero in Madison and Abner sometimes felt the weight of the added expectations associated with that relationship. Jonathan is now the Head Coach at McMichael High School which is the consolidated version of what used to be Madison/Mayodan High, and he has a son (Chris) who has also been a NCHSAA state champion during the last two years as a freshman and a sophomore.

At that time I had to use some pretty extreme measures to attempt to inspire Abner to be as physical as he was capable of being when he was at his best. In fact, he often reminds me of some of the degrees to which I went to get the good out of him. He will often say, "Do you remember when I was a junior and you had just got to Madison as the head coach and you took me down in that weight room and beat the crap out of me on the gymnastic mats and then you would just laugh about it like you thought something was funny." And then he will remind me about how much he improved during the two years that we worked together on the mat: "Now when I was a senior that wasn't so much fun for you was it coach?"

He is the real reason I got stuck with a title that has followed me all the way to Hendersonville. I guess I really was a little intensive and emotional during that first job as a wrestling coach and he began to call me "mad dog" behind my back, and sometimes to my face. And, I began to hear it everywhere I went. When I went to Hendersonville to coach, my new wrestlers would run into my old wrestlers at the state tournament and they would talk about how rough the practices had been and compare notes about their experiences. Abner had assigned me the title for life. I often say that even in my first job as an administrator, I knew I had arrived, and that I was getting the job done on the campus, when I noticed a rubbed out place on a hazy green door at the end of one of the buildings, that read "F--- You

MAD DOG." Abner's comment had sustained its life for over ten years.

But getting back to the phone call, when I picked up the phone, ten years after I had been his coach, Abner asked me to be the best man in his wedding. It was one of the greatest honors I have had since the day I decided to become a coach. My son who was three at the time and I packed up and returned to Madison for the wedding where we had a great time catching up on old times with Abner and his ushers, many of whom had also wrestled and played football for me back in the day. The depth of our respect for each other and our strong friendship evolved from the richness of the experiences we had during the work, the suffering and the triumphs that were generated on the mat. Abner is a very successful law enforcement agent in Rockingham County now. And he has a beautiful young family.

The relationships that are created in an elite wrestling program do not die at the graduation door. The successes, failures, extreme suffering, and excitement that are often experienced as a result of being a competitor, a coach, a statistician, or even a parent associated with an exceptional wrestling program tend to create bonds and memories that are with us forever.

The degree of intensity and personal investment required by wrestling often molds our lives and our relationships in ways that impact how we operate and work with others for the rest of our lives. There is almost always an element of pride, respect, and loyalty related to this sport that is embedded into who we are, how we frame the world, and what we value in the efforts of others.

West Henderson Wrestlers 1989. Left to right: Coach Darrell McDowell, Derek Irvin-2x state qualifier, Joe Arbogast-state qualifier, Kyle kuykendall-state champion, Todd Murphy 2x state qualifier, Troy Neil-state place winner, Stan Kumor state place winner, Brandon Cartee-state champion, Rob Atkinson-state champion.

There is a common respect that is found among people who truly understand the prices that have to be paid by wrestlers, coaches, parents, and yes, even officials, who support, promote and ensure the outstanding levels of participation and performance in the wrestling arena. This fraternal order appears to surpass boundaries such as differences in age or creed, whether it's high school, college, or "old timers." Differences in style, whether Greco-Roman, Freestyle, or Folkstyle, and variations with regard to State, National, and International Organizations do not appear to lessen the tremendous sense of uniformity with regard for the appreciation and respect found among almost all individuals who have been immersed in the purity of this sport, and the clarity of the work ethic that is essential to all successful wrestlers. Little has changed over the years with this element of the sport.

Jim Whitmer – All American at Appalachian State University in 1967.

The common price that has to be paid by all who enter the fraternity that is wrestling is ensured by sweat, blood, courage, toughness and sportsmanship. This investment pays dividends that include an eternal kinship and respect from all of those who have paid a similar price. Most wrestlers have gained the on-going advantage of utilizing a reservoir of experiences and relationships that can be used to compliment future challenges and enhance opportunities because of the characteristics they have developed through their participation in the sport.

11

Parental Support

I had been out of coaching for a couple of years. It was in
the mid 1990's, and I was acting as Assistant Principal at
East Henderson High School when I went over to the
NCHSAA Regional Tournament at Enka High School to
support our Eagle Wrestling Team. I was sitting in the upper
level of the bleachers watching a match that was going on
in one of the lower weight-classes. It was a hard fought and
emotional battle and the young man who lost, who I believe
was from Brevard High School, was clearly upset when the
other young man's hand was raised in victory. This is a
common occurrence. Nobody likes to lose. But what
happened next isn't common. As the upset young man
walked off the mat he was met by his mother who was even
more upset than he was about the outcome of the match.

As this episode began to unfold, it seemed as if it was
happening in slow motion. The mother of the loser stepped
over the roped off boundary and began to run across the
mat in front of a packed house full of wrestling fans. I
thought to myself, "this is not happening," "this is not
happening." And, then it happened. The boy's mother ran

across the mat full speed ahead and rammed Leigh Harris, the official, in the back, knocking him to his knees for a second. A group of coaches helped him back to his feet. He couldn't have been more sportsmanlike. He was just shocked by the incident. Other officials and coaches attempted to shield him from her verbal assaults as he gathered himself from the completely unprovoked, violent and ridiculous episode. She then picked up her bag and walked the full length of the gym in front of the crowd as they began to explode into a unified and powerful verbal cascade of "Boo's and yells." She then promptly turned and gave everyone in the arena the "Up Yours!" gesture as the security guards helped get her out of the building. You would have thought that you were at a WWE Professional Wrestling Event.

Fortunately, this is a very unique and unusual occurrence. But even the crazy folks do love their children and sometimes the emotions run high.

Wrestling parents find themselves in a unique position when their child decides to participate in an organized sport or activity. Often the depth and the necessity of accepting their responsibility for ensuring their own child's potential for success and participation is ignored or minimized. But a parent's perspective at the kitchen table, or comments made in the car on the way back from a practice or performance, can be used as an extreme opportunity to help their child, or lost as a missed chance to positively impact their life and their future.

Parents in the bleachers.

The extreme levels of work and time associated with wrestling offer continuous opportunities for parents to encourage and extend their child's personal levels of growth and maturity. Unfortunately, a percentage of parents, through no fault of their own, cannot give a legitimate perspective on eliminating the obstacles that come up with their child's feelings about their participation, and problems with performance in this sport. Parents are often placed at a disadvantage due to their lack of experience in wrestling. This is clearly another disadvantage that is not suffered to the same degree by the parents of children who choose to participate in one of the "big three" sports.

Almost everyone either knows someone in the neighborhood, or has someone in his family, who has played the revenue sports at some level. Many of our young people may even have access to the equipment needed to become familiar with those games. And most children have someone who can advise, or at least give an opinion, on the merits and advantages of participating in football, basketball, or baseball.

East Henderson High School Youth Football 2005.

Wrestling is a little different. Even though most of us grabbed our brothers and sisters and attempted to throw them to the ground in play, not many of us had the advantage of having access to coaches or wrestling mats until we were at a much older age than is experienced by children participating in football, basketball and baseball. Although some areas in the country have begun to develop recreational and youth wrestling programs that are beginning to enjoy significant popularity, it is important that coaches are aware of the obstacles that they will face as they begin to seek support and a level of confidence from parents. It is critical that strong lines of communication are kept open about the depth of the expectations that will be required by the athletes, and by the parents, that aspire to make a successful contribution to your wrestling program.

Further complicating the problems for parents are the obstacles related to weight loss and the maintenance of weight classes. This problem has been an issue throughout the history of the game. If there were easy answers to this issue, it would have been resolved long before now. Often parents have never been exposed to the levels of self-discipline that their children will begin to develop in many areas of their life as they begin to conform to the personal changes and dramatic regiments that are inevitably going to be experienced as they strive to become champions in wrestling.

Clearly, coaches and parents need to work together and always consider the physical and mental health of each child as a priority that would supersede any extreme effort to manipulate a child's bodyweight, whether that would include losing or gaining unreasonable weight percentages or pounds. Fortunately, most states have made exceptional efforts to build frameworks into their guiding rules and principles that would deter some of these problems. But, no matter what the issues are, parents are a tremendous factor in the success or failure of a coach's opportunity to provide successful instruction to their athletes and in helping to ensure the team's ability to win championships.

Parents would be well advised to develop a positive and welcoming relationship with their child's coaches, no matter what activity they are participating in as they develop toward adulthood. The biggest reason for that advice is to encourage the kind of relationships that will facilitate the best opportunities for wrestling parents to enjoy being a part of their children's lives, to the degree that they will be able to keep open lines of communication, and offer sound advice to their children when they are struggling with the work, their coach's demands, or problems that arise with their performance.

Parents would also reap healthy benefits from getting to know their coaches well enough to be comfortable asking questions that might help their child with any issues that come up during the season. Parents should also be prepared for relationships that will be constructed by their children with teammates and coaches that will be important and enduring as they begin committing and dedicating themselves to life as an amateur wrestler.

If real concerns come up about programs, practices, or policies related to the wrestling program, there are advantages to be enjoyed by all parties when parents attempt to work from a position of being on the same team, and attempting to work together on behalf of whatever is in the best interest of the child.

One other bit of advice to parents: wait until the next day following a match to approach the coach with questions and concerns. It is constructive for parents to make an appointment to meet with the coach about problems that come up, at a time other than during the match, or immediately following the contest. Both parties will make better decisions minus the adrenalin and the emotional climate of the heated post-match environment.

Most parents who commit to allowing their child to participate in wrestling, to the degree that they are a member of an elite or exceptional program, normally make an effort to become educated about the nature of the rules and the extreme amount of time and effort associated with the matches and tournaments in the sport. It is a very interesting process to watch, as the parents begin to learn the point system, the official's calls, the rules, and the overall parameters of a wrestling match. Whoever said a little bit of knowledge is a dangerous thing must have had the "rookie" wrestling parent in mind.

The emotionally charged parent is often unable to watch a match objectively. Parents tend to expend a level of energy that rivals that of the competitors on the mat, as they mentally wrestle each match right along with their child from their seat on the bleachers. Add to that the sensational and emotional dynamics that are often created in a live match scenario combined with an underdeveloped understanding of the rules, and it can make for an interesting evening of supervision and people watching. But normally, after a few weeks of listening, watching, and asking questions, parents actually do pretty well with educating themselves to a level of understanding that gives them a greater appreciation for their child's sport, the coach's job, and for the most part, they even learn to appreciate the officials.

Coaches would be well advised to utilize the outstanding resources that are included among your athlete's parents. Very few parents are not motivated to make some kind of contribution toward enhancing the opportunities for their child and his teammates. Some are even willing to make exceptional contributions to your wrestling program because they have a sincere appreciation for the tremendous sacrifices that you will make as a successful championship-caliber wrestling coach.

To help ensure your status with parents and the community, plan to initiate an early coach's meeting where you can go over the rules, set expectations for student and parent performance, and illustrate parameters for adult sportsmanship. This small, but obliging element of communication will pay tremendous dividends as you work with them in your program throughout the rest of the season and the remainder of their child's career.

Parents should never be allowed to dictate how you run your program. You are, and should be, the expert. But, a failure to give them an open ear, arranged and defined by your terms, may create an environment that limits a chance to have them contribute toward the success of their child, or your program, which creates an unfortunate result for all parties.

A related issue for both parents and coaches includes coming to an objective understanding about their child's ability-something many parents are incapable of. This is not unique to our sport. But, the sooner you serve this reality onto the table of discussions with parents the better off you and the program will be.

This lack of objectivity on the part of some parents will eventually erupt to the forefront at some point during your tenure as a wrestling coach, and usually at some point during each season. It is far better to openly this difficult issue than to avoid it. Even the mothers and fathers who may work closely with your program may need to be reminded of how difficult it will be for them to view their child's performance through an unbiased lens.

The relationships that coaches develop with parents can be very beneficial when dealing with a wide variety of scenarios that arise from the peaks of victory and the ashes of defeat in this business. Parents that were formerly wrestlers can become a tremendous asset to your program. They often bring tradition, pride, loyalty, understanding, and a helpful framework of stability to your overall population of parents. On the other hand, you had no part in the kind of experience they enjoyed, or endured, in their own wrestling career. Their perception of "how we ought to do things around here" may be clouded by bad experiences suffered during their days on the mat. Or even worse, parents may attempt to live vicariously through their children. The latter is usually the most difficult of the potential scenarios. When a parent is trying to live out what they accomplished, or what they failed to accomplish when they were on a team, it can lead to a variety of dynamics, none of which are usually very good for the wrestler, and even worse for your program.

Darrell McDowell, West Henderson High School – Coach Cliff Wilson vs. Jerome Conley, Brevard – Coach Tim Ellenberger, 1979 Conference Tournament at Brevard.

The range of problems with some parents can start with a child quitting the team under the pressure of unrealistic expectations on the part of an overbearing parent who either has no experience on the mat or has a misguided notion about what it takes to be successful. This can be a tremendous burden that eventually leads to disappointment and a hard landing for that wrestler, and for all who are associated with ensuring that particular child's success. There are numerous scenarios that fall within this range of possibilities that are experienced on either side of the situations mentioned above.

12

The Purity of the Process

*T*he most difficult experience that I ever suffered through
while coaching happened in February of 1989. The
1988 team had finished fourth in the state tournament and
we were loaded with a large number of well-skilled
returning athletes on the West Henderson wrestling team.
From about the 112lb. weight class through 189lbs. we were
stacked with solid kids. We had sent ten wrestlers to the
state tournament in the year before and most of them were
back. In December one of my 145lb. wrestlers injured his
knee and while he was out another of my excellent athletes
dropped into the weight class to fill the empty spot. By the
time they were both healthy each of them had excellent
winning percentages, though neither had an exceptional
number of matches for the entire year.

Todd Murphy was a senior and had been a very solid
performer in the years that preceded his last. In fact he was
a three time conference champion and a state qualifier who
had won several matches in Chapel Hill during his junior
year. The other student was Kyle Kuykendall. He was
undefeated in the matches that he had wrestled during the
year in question and showed great promise as being a very

qualified young competitor. Unfortunately neither had been able to qualify to drop to 140 and neither could move up and compete at the 152 pound weight class. This might appear to be a good problem, but the scenario eventually became pure misery for all of us.

I would be forced to make the most difficult decision that I had ever made in my coaching career. There was a part of me that truly thought that the right thing to do would have been to let the senior who had paid so many dues and contributed so much over the past three years to automatically get the chance to return to the state tournament for the second year. But in reality the decision about who competes had to be made before the regional qualifying tournament. The politics and opinions were on high among team members, families, and anyone who was even aware of the dilemma I was about to face with two young men that I had grown to love like my own sons. It might have been easier if at least one of them had been a hoodlum or a thug. But, they were perfect gentlemen and exceptional student/citizens. They both had the work ethic of a soldier and the loyalty of a family member.

Knowing the serious loss that would eventually be suffered by one of these wonderful young men, I determined that I would have a series of wrestle-offs that would decide who would compete in the regional and possibly the state tournament. The first man to secure two victories would represent our school in the region. In the first match the elder Todd won by one point. In the second match Kyle won by one point. It was at this point that I eliminated myself from the process. I had officiated both of the first two matches. I made the decision to hire the most respected official in the mountains at that time to come to the school to preside over the last match of the series. We met at Rugby middle School and used their full size mat and gym to determine who would move on. Tim Ellenberger, a friend and a top notch referee, was gracious enough to volunteer his time to officiate this unbelievably emotional contest.

Watching the match, coaching neither of the wrestlers, was the most excruciating experience I had ever had within the boundaries of a team situation. When the final whistle had blown Kyle Kuykendall had defeated the elder Todd Murphy in another emotionally draining one point match that left us all near tears. And we would have felt equally burdened by either outcome. Todd's career was ended on that mat on that day in an intensive and competitive environment that might as well have been the state finals as far as any of us were concerned.

Kyle qualified for the state tournament and had some difficulty with his level of performance. But during the next year with the experience that he had gained and without the struggle he had suffered to get past Todd Murphy, Kyle went on to become a NCHSAA State Champion at the 160lb. weight class in 1990. He later went on to win a Southern Conference Title for Appalachian State University four years after he won the NC State Tournament. Kyle now works as a Law Enforcement agent in Charlotte NC.

As for Todd, he was a gentlemen and a good sport about his unfortunate situation. His parents on the other hand did not embrace my remedy for deciding who would compete in the regional and state tournament that year. When senior night came to West Henderson shortly after the wrestle-off, Todd's parents publicly refused to shake my hand as we gave them their flower and thanked them for the help they had provided for our program over the years. I know they hurt for their son and it was difficult for all of us. I never took it personally. I did what I knew I had to do with the situation. And I didn't really expect that everyone would agree with it. But everyone did not have to live with it either. In this sport, big decisions need to be decided on the mat.

Since that time I have spoken often with Todd's mother and father. They are wonderful people. None of us chose to have to endure that time of difficulty, but we all got through it. Since that time I have bought a couple of cars from Todd's father at the dealership where he works and his mother is a teacher in our school system. Todd went on to become a teacher and he coaches at Hendersonville Middle School. He has been a successful addition to the school and to the community. In fact, he has coached against my son who wrestled for Rugby Middle School on several occasions. He has always been a fine young man. And this is a small and ironic world.

There is hope and a sound solution for resolving many of the problems that can arise in wrestling programs that do not often exist in other sports. Coaches must aspire to cling tightly to the essence of what has kept this athletic event as pure as it has been able to remain over the many years of strenuous participation.

Fortunately, even in the face of all who would contort the framework of wrestling to their own political satisfaction, or to their child's advantage, their remains the essential equalizing component of wrestle-offs and challenge matches that purify the process. Much of the previously discussed misfortune endured by wrestlers and their coaches can be cleared up on the mat. Yes, there will always be close matches that are decided wrongly by misjudged calls on the part of the officials. But those incidences are rare. If wrestlers commit themselves to the work, and to understanding and obtaining the necessary knowledge from coaches, teammates, and competitors, while believing in their own abilities, there is always a clear avenue of opportunity for success in wrestling.

The biggest mistake coaches can make that affects the continuity of their program would be to hand pick line-ups for competition, based what they only presume about the talents of their athletes. Coaches that disallow individual opportunity for self-promotion to starting positions by all team members deface the credibility of their own process and confuse the ambition of both the coach and the program. Embrace the wrestle-off procedure. There are few structures left in life that adhere to the cleanliness and clarity that are identified with this important selection framework.

The most common mistakes that are made with this type of structure occur when, as mentioned earlier, an up-coming younger wrestler attempts to challenge a senior's position as they develop and move toward the end of the season. This transition of power or status can and will occur if you stay in the business long enough. This is probably one of the most difficult scenarios to deal with as the leader, and a model for your program. But in reality, the better man should always have the opportunity to progress forward.

One way to ensure that the best man actually represents the program is to settle the issue with the best two out-of-three challenge matches. This can be a very tough time, and an unsettling scenario for wrestlers, coaches, and parents. Most parents of the senior student will be reluctant to accept this solution for arriving at a fair resolution, especially if their child is eliminated from a chance to participate in the State Tournament.

It is never easy, and it may be as painful for the coach as it is for either the parent or the student. But coaching is a tough and unforgiving business at times, and you have to be in charge of many difficult propositions. Do not expect that you will feel absolutely comfortable with every decision that you have to make. But this is one area where you should establish the parameters for this situation long before it arises by detailing the process at the pre-season meeting, so that the senior and the challenging youth can prepare for this potential collision in the early stages of this journey.

13

Organizing Your Program for a Successful Season

West Henderson High School Team Picture, 1989.

*A*bout three years into my coaching experience at West Henderson we began to develop a strong foundation of well-equipped kids that were competitive with almost any of the teams in North and South Carolina. But it was getting near November as I looked over the roster and it was clear *that we had no one that would be able to get down to a healthy weight that would even near the 103lb. class. It is difficult to start every match of the season forfeiting that first weight class to every opponent. So I was on the hunt.*

I began to look throughout the student body and there was hardly anyone walking the halls of the school that even looked that small. And, then it happened. I was in the cafeteria at lunch one day and I noticed this really underdeveloped young fellow. He was a gangly looking, skinny little guy who just did not look the part. He did appear to be light enough in pounds, but he was so physically immature that I hesitated to even ask if he might consider coming out for the team. In fact, I didn't ask. I just said "what's your name" and he said in some type of upper midwest accent, "Mike Morris." And then I said "Mike you're going to be my 103lb. pound wrestler this year." He began to state that he didn't know anything about wrestling. So I of course began to launch into one of my better speeches about what it could mean for him and more importantly what it could mean for our team and our school. He sort of half-heartedly agreed to show up at practice to see if it might be something he could do. Honestly, I was a little worried about his physical capacity to endure what would be in store for him, especially with the room full of animals that we had that year.

He did come to practice that day and it was pretty ugly at first. I know he was scared to death by his teammates and my aggressive style of coaching. But, he hung in there. Some of the kids seemed to really take to him. I think some of them felt sorry for him and some just knew how desperately we needed someone to fill that gap at 103. He had to hit the ground running because it was overall an advanced group of kids that year. But I began to see a level of hope in his performance. He was a yes sir, no sir kid who would attempt to wade into the deep end for you, even though it was really over his head a lot of the time. With his unusually flexible and brittle looking appearance, he was often referred to as our newborn calf at the beginning of the season.

Our first dual match that year was away at Tuscola High School in Waynesville NC. Everybody was cranked up and we finally located a singlet that was small enough to fit him. He was visibly nervous about stepping out on the mat in his first competition. The introductions were made and a couple of preliminary matches were wrestled and then it was time for Michael to go on the mat. As the first period progressed I was absolutely hopeful about his chances to survive all three periods. I was beginning to get that proud feeling about what kind of job I had done with this green little fellow when the unexpected happened.

When the whistle blew to end the first period the official said "your choice green" and Michael looked over at me. I said, "defer the choice." The Tuscola kid said "I'll take top." I said, "Michael get in the down position." It was at that point when things got really interesting. Rather than placing his knees on one side of the double lines and his hands on the other, he straddled both lines. The double lines ran between his arms at one end of his body and between his legs on the other end. And that would have been bad enough, but when he was asked to correct the position, he turned a complete 180 degrees and faced the opposite wrong direction. I guess I sort of went off the deep end as I yelled to try and fix him, a little embarrassed for him and me, because about that time a couple of parents from Tuscola yelled down to the mat and told me to shut up and leave the poor kid alone. I wanted to get mad, but I couldn't because inside I was laughing so hard. In fact at that point we all began laughing out loud as we finally got him straightened out in his position. Michael didn't win that match. But this unlikely start was just the beginning for him.

He accumulated a fierce work ethic during the next three years. He used a savage approach to learning the game and developing the kind of body that could endure the punishment and deliver the skill level that he would eventually obtain. Mike went on during his junior and senior years to qualify for the state tournament where he won three matches as a senior. Mike gained a level of superior performance, beating many quality opponents that year. I am as proud of that young man as any I have ever coached. He still loves the game and he has utilized that work ethic to ensure his success in the business world in Raleigh. He has a beautiful family and very successful career.

I learned a hard lesson that night. Don't assume anything. No matter how good you think you may be. Never forget the fundamentals and the details as you plan for your practices and for your season.

⊙⊙⊙

An effort to dictate every detail of how to ensure a uniform plan that can be initiated in exact duplication in every wrestling program, at every school, or situation, would be a presumptuous mistake. In fact, it is probably impossible to expect to use one prescription for building a program to meet the needs of any two coaching positions.

Organizing Your Program for a Successful Season

The differences in communities, schools, and the various skill levels of coaches and kids, along with a wide array of varying individual characteristics, will either contribute or detract from what you will be able to utilize for success. You will need to begin to organize and discriminate between the benefits of the tools that will be mentioned in the following sections of this book, embracing the practices and methods that fit well with your previous experiences. It is important that you feel confident about the instructional process that you will need to use to meet the needs of your individual situation, while shelving anything that you might feel would be better suited in a situation somewhere else.

The ideas and experiences related to developing an elite wrestling program that are illustrated in the following material should provide many possibilities for infusing life, vision, and stability into your program. This philosophy and system for developing a successful wrestling program has proven to be very effective in more than one coaching scenario. And it is likely that many of the methods and program details discussed can be modified and adjusted to meet the needs of your team, their parents, the community, and the other stake-holders associated with your overall program.

The most important job you will have, in the initial stages of establishing your team as a head wrestling coach, will be to create a vision for your program. It will be your responsibility to clearly illustrate, in detail, what you expect from each wrestler, and where you expect the program to go, today, tomorrow, and three years from now.

One of the biggest mistakes that you can make as a new coach is to <u>assume</u> anything about what you might think your wrestler's goals are, or what you may think they have prescribed for themselves, or to leave it to them as youths to decide what they think they will need to do to be able to contribute to your program. The map that you will have to develop for them to help ensure a successful journey on this road to exceptional performance and championship rewards will have to be visualized, illustrated, and sold to your wrestlers in increments of inches, yards, and miles, if you expect to excel to the upper levels of amateur wrestling performance.

The vision that you will have to use to ensure success for your team will often have to include thorough, and sometimes tedious, descriptions of where your wrestlers are going, why they are going there, why they should want to go, and how you're going to help them get to the State Championship Tournament. Yes, it will eventually be up to each individual wrestler, after intensive instruction and conditioning, to take responsibility for reaching the ultimate destination of personal and team goals. But as you pursue excellence in your program, it will be your job as the coach to model, encourage, and demand an adherence to the expectations set forth by the standards that you lay out for your team.

Coach Wally Burke, High Point Andrews "Providing a vision."

It is a mistake to assume that any of your wrestlers are going to love wrestling as much as you do. Some of them will eventually love it more than you do, if you create a rich environment of success, fellowship and tradition. But for you to presume that they will have a level of inspired ambition, and fundamental skill at their various levels of development as a young man, or woman, is a mistake that can have dire consequences with regard to their self-imposed limitations, and the potential negative impact that can be cast on the success of your team without attention to this reality.

Clearly written, and carefully constructed expectations, and detailed descriptions of the technical strategies, will be essential to move the entire program forward. Your high level of energy, enthusiasm, and extreme framework of demands, early in the birth of your program, will help drive the vision of what you must prescribe for your team's success. You will need to energetically clarify, illustrate, and burn your detailed expectations into the minds of your wrestlers.

One way to ensure that wrestlers attend to establishing championship oriented, program-acceptable goals is to have each wrestler write them down on a sheet of paper and have them schedule an individual meeting to talk to you as the Head Coach about their vision for the season. They will need to verbalize and discuss what their personal goals are, and define how they intend to pursue them with some ambition, and with guidance from you.

To accentuate the importance and the value attached to your objectives you will need to demand that they keep this list of goals with them, in their wallet, and you will need to ask them to periodically review and modify them to adjust to their improved levels of performance. Tell them ahead of time that you may request to see their personal document at a moment's notice, on the bus, on the way to a match, at a restaurant on the way home, or it may be after practice as they walk by your office door. But this simple and tangible method for attaching a level of importance to the need to create and embrace a clearly paved avenue for striving for championship goals will enhance their level of vision and their potential for participating in their own individual achievement.

Unless you are currently coaching at the college level, you probably won't be able to recruit athletes outside of your school or organization. The students that you have in your building will be the only ones you're going to get. I will qualify this statement by saying that you need to do a good job recruiting the best people you can get from your current population of students.

As your program grows, and you begin to find success in the years to come, your recruiting job will normally get to be a little easier. In fact, according to the degree to which you find success, especially if you are able to establish a dynasty, a number of parents may even make a change in residence to live in your community, based on the opportunities your program can offer their child as a member of an elite wrestling team. But, the creativity and work ethic in this game can be used to allow you to utilize the individuals that you already have on your squad to find a way to compete, even in the early days of your coaching career.

More important than the types of players you end up with will be what you have to say, and do, to capitalize on the potential talents that each young individual will bring to the table. As they commit their varying body types and hopes to your program, it will be your job to have the high expectations and to dig out the strengths that will be embedded deep within their hearts, bodies, and souls. You must find ways to motivate an extreme level of commitment from each wrestler, one that will extend their capacities beyond what their preconceived ideas and accepted limitations about themselves have suppressed and limited to this point in their lives.

Another important element that goes hand-in-hand with preconceived ideas about your program will be associated with the personal attitudes of your students with regard to how they perceive what it means to be a wrestler, and more importantly, what it means to be a wrestler in your program, and on your particular team. This will be an important issue for you, as coach, to address. The culture of the program affects every aspect of your potential success on a day-to-day basis. Your athletes need to understand how a wrestler in your program is suppose to look, act, and be, so that they can begin to strive to acquire those identified traits and know how to meet your expectations.

If you are in a new coaching position where much success in wrestling has preceded your tenure as the new man at the helm, you will need to capitalize on some of the traditions that were established in this winning program. If there is evidence that your athletes are educated to any degree, with effective fundamental skills, that appear to be in line with your ambition and objectives, you may be able to capitalize on their familiarity as a starting place to generate a foundation to take the program to even greater heights of success in a shorter amount of time than if you had to start from the ground up. If the team has already has a strong tradition it is likely that there will already be some former coaching and wrestling heroes in the community that will help ensure a level of history and enthusiasm from the past team's successes that can help make your job easier when it comes time to recruit.

But, be wise about how you embrace this situation. Yes, you will need to establish your own level of hierarchy and personal structure as the Head Coach. And, as the new leader in the wrestling community at your school, the natural tendency on your part may be to attempt to erase the old ways of doing things. You may feel the need to change everything in an effort to highlight the goals and the structure of your new ideas and expectations by contrasting differences in methods and styles of performance on the backs of the old way, and at the expense of tearing down any of ideas that might be left over from the old regime. But it doesn't always have to be out with the old, and in with the new, especially if the former coaching staff had some success and was fundamentally sound with their approach to the game.

Sometimes, especially in our youth, as coaches, we make mistakes in our new roles that are initiated out of a simple lack of experience with dealing with people in a professionally competitive environment. Don't be insecure about giving credit to the former staff. Your confirmation about the quality of the former Head Coach will not limit what you have to offer your wrestlers. And keep in mind that students, and sometimes parents, will still make critical and hurtful comments related to your coaching efforts, as exceptional as they may be. They are often motivated by a selfish, or just a naïve and uninformed failure to understand or appreciate your hard work.

You will eventually gain the benefit of growing a thick skin, and finding diplomatic ways of educating. You will have future opportunities to display the exceptional worth of your plan, and you will be able to highlight and establish the value that you will bring to their lives as their new coach.

Encourage your wrestlers to do some wrestling in the off-season. Many will be self-motivated about finding avenues to get back on the mat when the regular season is over. One effective way to help ensure the success of students who want to pursue more mat time can be found by encouraging them to participate in Club Wrestling Programs. They are starting to pop up all over the state and the nation. Be wise about analyzing the ambition of the club's vision for their athletes and it would probably be helpful to become involved in the club to some degree to help motivate and monitor the progress of their off-season efforts.

In North Carolina two particular individuals come to mind that have laid a lot of groundwork for ensuring the success of Club Programs. Norman Osteen, who established the Strong and Courageous Wrestling Club, has been very successful over the years with assisting in the development of many kids in the Western part of North Carolina. And Mike Kendall, North Carolina's first four-time NCHSAA State Champion from Albemarle High School, has worked with many athletes in the eastern part of the state in a club called The Cardiac Kids. Kendall recently worked as the Head Coach at Chapel Hill High School, and he has now accepted the job as the Head Coach at East Wake High School near Raleigh, North Carolina.

Norman Osteen was instrumental at North Henderson High School during the early 1990's, along with Head Coach Barry Bonnet as they led North Henderson to their only State Tournament Championship Title. Norman has been a Head Coach at the High School level at East Henderson High School and he assisted at Gardner Webb University. He has participated in helping coach several nationally ranked wrestling athletes in the amateur wrestling arena. Both Osteen and Kendall have been enthusiastic participants on the club scene and have made successful contributions to improving the skill level of many athletes who have competed successfully in the state, and in the nation.

Coach Norman Osteen and Joe Shively, Strong and Courageous Wrestling Club. Joe is also the starting 103lb. wrestler for Mark Harris as a freshman at Enka High School.

Each high school coach should assess the integrity of the club organizations that are available in their local areas and make a distinction about what would be the best and most effective scenario for ensuring their off-season expectations for their wrestlers. But the club competitions should definitely be a part of that consideration. Some athletes participate in a broad number of sports. But for those who choose to concentrate on one sport, club wrestling can be a very beneficial avenue for improving individual skills and obtaining precious mat time.

Brantley Hooks is a 2x South Carolina State Champion from Byrnes High School and he is a Strong and Courageous Club Competitor. Brantley is coached by Eric Hansen on his high school team and Norman Osteer in the club. Brantley will wrestle in college for Don Wirnberger at Bucknell University.

14

From the Ground Up

*A*bout three weeks into my first season as the head wrestling coach West Henderson High School it was about 7:30 p.m. and I was heading toward my car on the lighted and covered sidewalk in front of the main office of the school. I saw a man in a suit and tie headed in my direction and I began to recognize that it was one of my former elementary school principal's from Etowah Elementary School. His name was Malvern or "Buddy" West and he was still the school leader at that same site where my mother, myself, and eventually all of my three children would go to school in the years to come, none of which was by design. Mr. West had also gone to grade school with my dad. I had already heard many war stories about what a "handful" my dad had been in school and what a headache Grady had been for some of the teachers in his day.

As we squared up in the light on the sidewalk Mr. West asked me how I was doing in my new job and he then asked me "what are you doing over here?" And I said what do you mean?" He then said I'm hearing some pretty severe comments about what you're putting these boys through on *the wrestling team. He said he had heard that we had been going three or four hours with practice and that some of them were having a hard time making it and that some of them had even quit. My answer was "well almost everything you've said is true." He truly meant to be helpful as he said that I needed to be careful about the degree to which I was pushing these young men. But, he had no idea about the rewards that would follow this gauntlet of emotion and toughness. And, he also had no idea how this community would embrace the results of the ambitious efforts of those who fully committed themselves to this dream.*

Some coaches would fear the most challenging opportunity to take over a wrestling program. The coaching jobs that come open, more often than not, are in schools where there has been a lack of success. In many districts, the same coaching positions tend to come open on a regular basis, every two or three years. Sometimes these losing situations are generated due to a lack of administrative or community support. Many times they continue to exist due to an administrative history that appears to have little interest in searching out a competent candidate. Or it may be that no wrestling culture has ever been established at the school because the "right" person has never been hired.

Well-equipped coaches with a desire to engage in a challenge should not be fearful of this scenario. In fact, this may be a prime opportunity. The only real necessity that should be at least considered, if you are planning to take over a high school team, is that there will be a need to establish a feeder program at the middle school. Long-term success can be enhanced tremendously with the potential to establish fundamental correctness at the lower levels of performance. But with that in place, the rewards that you will receive as an empire builder can become an extraordinary experience for you, the wrestlers, and for the community.

If, however, a new coach starts at a school with a losing history, taking over the ailing coaching situation may require a more dramatic, and sometimes traumatic, approach. The methods will be somewhat foreign, and may seem extreme compared to what has been accepted as a legitimate practice session in the past. The intensive nature of the work and the time devoted to changing the overall wrestling climate will likely be an unfamiliar and shocking experience for the returning wrestlers and their parents.

Each coach will have their own personality and philosophy that will contour the overall direction of their new program. But all will have to establish a common belief, and a confidence in the methods, or tools, that are offered as they attempt to prepare to go to "war" on the mat. Keep in mind that most athletes who have been participating in an unsuccessful program will not even understand this metaphoric and intensive illustration of competing. The most difficult and important element of selling your brand of success will be found in your efforts to destroy the negative obstacles that have been welded into the minds of each wrestler, and into the community, about what it has meant to be identified as a loser in the sport and what it will take to rise from these ashes.

A large part of your new job will include finding ways to extinguish all the negative baggage that interrupts the flow of consistent confidence building that will occur as they begin to acquire the benefits of becoming fundamentally sound. Some things will become absolutely unacceptable during practice sessions. The words "I can't" or "I'm tired" have to become taboo among the wrestling team members. They will need to traded in for terms such as "suck it up!" or "you can do anything full speed for six minutes of your life" will need to become commonplace in this new kind of environment that lends itself to building a winning culture.

Initially, you will have to challenge individual students that appear to fall short of mental and physical expectations during practice sessions. The term "shaming them into performing" is probably a little strong with regard to pushing wrestlers past what they believe are their limits. But, whatever you say to them, within reasonable terms, will not compare to the bewilderment and potential embarrassment that they can expect to endure on the mat if they approach the game with the wrong attitude. It is your responsibility to create an environment in the practice room that will closely resemble the intensive, sometimes hostile, realities that will inevitably be faced in wrestling competition.

Some coaches might say, "It is not my job to teach attitude." Almost certainly, these coaches will be losers. It is without a doubt and absolutely your continuous job to teach attitude. And it is best taught by example. It can, and should, be modeled by you. It may be in a practice session when one of your own wrestlers decides to take on a leadership role, or it may have to be modeled, or revealed early in the process by the posture and composure of a respected opponent.

Your kids need to see that you value positive and determined attitudes; even if it means that they have to first see you congratulate, or compliment, a competitor on another team for an exceptional performance. Keep in mind that sometimes an exceptional performance doesn't always include a win. And it is your job to have the expertise and the wrestling knowledge to understand and reward the exceptional and successful performances of your athletes. This is especially important in the early days of developing a positive climate in your program. At first, the wins may be few and far between.

Wrestlers need to know that you care about what they do, about their individual levels of improvement, about their needs as individual human beings and about their role as a valued team member. You will be able to push your athletes through enormous amounts of work and extreme levels of performance if they know that you are just as willing to go to the same degree to help them with whatever they need, on or off the mat.

Jerry Winterton, Head Coach of Cary High School encouraging and instructing his wrestler. Photo provided by David Maney II, Sports Information Director

Practice sessions can go in any direction that you want them to go. Many adults that aspire to coach do not choose to understand, and almost always understate, the reality that you will get whatever you ask for as a result of what you prescribe as the head coach. If you claim that you don't accept excuses from your wrestlers, then you better begin

98

by making none for yourself. Yes, you will be limited to some degree, for a short time, due to the caliber of your initial athletes. But it is your job to create wrestlers. Talent is important, but it has less to do with the final product in your program than the parameters that you have set for ensuring success, especially in this diverse and creative sport of wrestling.

15

Practice

When I left Madison/Mayodan after three years as the head coach, I had made my share of mistakes as a twenty-two to twenty-five year-old. And I had learned several lessons about coaching in the process. I had also won a conference championship and had sixty-four kids on the team during my last year there. I had gained the advantage of competing in a league that was beneficial about preparing me to be ready to compete in the mountains. The consistent competition of the Greensboro area heightened my sense of understanding about what I would have to do to compete at the state level when I returned to an ailing situation with the wrestling program at my alma mater.

Sadly, three of my Madison/Mayodan wrestlers including: Anthony Gann, John Garner and Mark Friddle helped me move my family to the mountains in a U-haul that I rented in Rockingham County before I left the town of Madison. All three of those guys and several others went on to place in the state tournament in the year following my departure. It was a very bittersweet time as I made the transition back to my hometown.

When the season started at West Henderson during my first year back to Henderson County, I was equipped to meet the challenge of enhancing the program, but I had an overwhelming sense of ambition about avoiding failure at the high school I had attended. I had no lack of emotion or vision about what I wanted. But the success of the struggling team would be determined by my potential to communicate that vision to a bunch of young men who hadn't seen a falcon wrestler qualify for the state tournament in five years. My work was cut out for me and I had no false impression about the situation that I was in with the program.

I recruited hard and there were a few young men like Brian Cartee and Rick Atkinson that I could not have run off with a horse whip. But even while recruiting, I saw some signs of apprehension and a naïve perception of what some of them thought practice might include when it come to the demands that would be inflicted on their efforts to produce.

On the day I met with them to make my speech and unveil my vision for the next four months of their life, I did it from the top of the teacher desk in the Health Room located near the gym. You can call it shock value, eccentric behavior or just an unbelievable desire to have their attention as we began to mold a common vision for the program, but apparently it was effective. I started on one side of the black board noting their expected path from that very day in November and I painted a picture of each detailed expectation for the season that ended at the other side of the black board with a clear expectation noted about a trip to Chapel Hill at the state tournament, something that none of them had ever attended before that year, and certainly none had ever participated in as a competitor. But when I was finished with what I had to say, no one in the room could have any question about how real my expectations were for making this journey a reality.

They could not really envision how severe that first year of practices would be in terms of mental, physical and emotional expectations, but fortunately for me most of them bought into my plan. We had three young men that made it to the state tournament in Chapel Hill that year and we had ten that qualified the next year.

I am often reminded of that day when I projected everything that I could to muster up a clear vision for our new program from the top of that desk. I know some of them thought I was little crazy that first day in the Health Room and I'm not sure that was a bad thing. But none of them have ever questioned or denied my enthusiasm for ensuring their potential as a wrestler or as a young man.

Developing a successful practice session requires planning, organizing, and direction. As in any organization, there will be some things that you will like to do, and others that need to be done. It doesn't make any sense to develop a practice schedule because you think you ought to be doing what everybody else does. Sure, we have all stolen ideas and technical expertise from other teams. But your practices need to be designed with a successful end in mind. Watching film, scouting other teams, executing superior challenge matches, and identifying strengths and weaknesses on a daily, weekly, monthly and yearly basis will all be some of the most important aspects of your preparation to compete successfully.

As you begin to develop your schedule for the year, you will need to consider your returning technical skill levels and athletic prowess. You will need to develop a schedule that will challenge your wrestlers to the extent of their potential. Do not be afraid to travel miles and distance to ensure a chance to compete with the best. If you are limited by the level of competition that exists in your particular state or demographic location, you better develop the kind of relationship with your school administration that will give the freedom you will need to travel to where the competition exists, whether it is in-state, or out. If you must err in your scheduling, let it be on the side of a challenge that is too great, rather than too weak.

Before you ever begin your first practice, keep in mind that nothing you will be able to do physically will be accomplished until you establish the mental and emotional parameters and expectations for your team. If you have taken the challenge of becoming the leader of a formerly weak program, it may mean that you have to take them to the Health Room, or another classroom environment in your school, stand on top of the desk for emphasis, and break out in a visionary sermon that establishes what you want the team to accomplish for the year. I did. You may have to draw a framework on the chalk board that details a persistent and progressive line of ambition and perspective that disallows any negative possibility that might creep into the year's strategic plan for ensuring individual wins, conference championships, or state tournament expectations.

Often this first meeting will reveal a prescription for them and you. For many, it is this initial unveiling of the work that will have to be done that will highlight their individual attitudes, both good, and bad, with regard to the compressed and intensive journey that lies ahead in the description of the plan. Utilize this rich orientation into the program to begin to establish expectations and values for your team. Some may quit the team after the meeting is over. They may pack their bags and go home at the conclusion of your comments. And, they may very well be making the best decision for everyone involved if there appears to be a lack of commitment, after hearing the expected mental and physical costs demanded by your program.

This can often happen if you have been absolutely clear about what will be expected of them as a member of your program. But after the first year, this should become an unusual occurrence. Your individual practices should reflect what you have clarified with your wrestlers in this meeting. Your athletes should leave this initial skull session feeling a sense of pride and ambition about being challenged and ready to go to work.

Head coach Jerry Winterton, Cary High School, giving his version of a preparatory "Team Speech." Photo provided by David Maney II, CHS Sports Information Director.

Practice

When the first day of practice arrives make sure that mats are clean, statisticians and managers are in place and expectations about being on time and warming up are established immediately. Your practices should begin to generate a familiar pace and rhythm to the daily process. The purposeful surprises that you will integrate into the normal routine, as you need to change their skill level and improve their performance, will be more effectively introduced in a stable framework of daily procedures. New information should be introduced with clear objectives that answer, not only the "what" of what you intend to teach, but also the "why" of what you are teaching.

Once your team members begin to rise to your level of expectations for intensive performance, use individual wrestlers to help set the pace with demonstrating new techniques and reinforce consistent models throughout the teaching and drilling sessions. This will often inspire leadership roles and responsibilities that will begin to rapidly evolve in the practice setting. If you have coaches that are well skilled and physically fit, or if you choose to be a hands-on participant in the practice sessions, you may be able to help establish your expectations about necessary levels of performance by modeling, demonstrating and generating the mental, physical, and emotional parameters that have to be associated with the game.

At some time during the middle of the season, in the practice process, especially following the successful acquisition of superior physical conditioning and an improved level of skillful technical expertise, your wrestlers will begin to take pride in their work and expect to be pushed to their limits.

In fact, you will begin to find that your leaders on the team may begin to challenge each other, and they may even challenge you. As the season goes forward, you may choose to strategically lighten the volume of physical combat in practices to help manage the flow of needed recuperation time or change certain technical aspects of the process that veer from the established plan. These kinds of unusual circumstances may inspire the exceptional and more mature individuals in your program to ask you why you are deviating from what they expect from a practice session. Don't be alarmed by this reaction.

Whether you know it or not, you have begun the process of developing a young man. This increased level of confidence should, in some way, be rewarded unless it is done out of the bounds of respectfulness. But more likely than not, you will know that in most cases, he is aspiring to be affirmed and respected, even if your response has to finally end up being, "I'm the coach and you're the wrestler and the final responsibility lies with me," he will appreciate the fact that he was treated like a respected part of the organization to that point in his engagement. Only you will be able to determine what his motives are, and you will have to act accordingly. Just make sure you are really listening to what he is saying, especially when he has consistently conformed to your previous expectations.

Eventually everyone in the practice room, if he is able to remain on the team and become a respected part of the program, will begin to understand what is really going on. The experience begins to reveal that it has less to do with wrestling, and more to do with pushing the boundaries of each young man's personal ambitions. It is about preparing them for life. The sweat, the blood, and the tears are a prescribed microcosm of how they will begin to operate as they face their opponents on the mat and if necessary in the world. Other more important events will surely come that will require a heightened level of awareness and engagement, both on the mat and off.

Often in a high intensity practice room, coaches inspire ongoing challenges by making connections to real life, motivating students with comments such as, "You think this is tough, what are you going to do one of these days when them babies gotta eat?" Or, "it's just a little blood, there's more where that came from," or "it's just a finger. You got nine more," or "You better not even sleep on your back during this season." These kinds of comments may sound a little extreme to some of you. But, in the wrestling environment, the demands are high, and so is the level of pride and expectation.

Bringing a boom box or music system into the practice room can be an effective way to motivate performance that can also be carried over into warm-up drills at home matches. It can become a part of the traditional routine that inspires a general sense of comfort and a familiar escalation of motivation toward the competition.

This musical interlude tends to establish and stabilize a sense of identity and a strong posture for the team's overall persona that adds to what often ends up being a unifying element of the pre-contest drama. It is not a necessity for some people. But it has already paid exceptional dividends to an increasing number of programs and their level of success.

Most teams will choose an agreed upon song or rhythm to use for warm-up drills at home matches. The music is inspiring, contemporary, emotionally strong, and moving songs that enhance a pumped up and aggressive environment. It is fine, even preferred, that wrestlers help put the songs together as a team. Keep the lyrics clean and ensure that the music is an empowering culmination of dramatic compositions that help to promote a progressive flow of focus, and enhance the vision for your program. And you may just find that practice becomes more intensive, more fun, and you might even help ensure a level of mutual respect between you and your dedicated warriors.

Young people are smart. They miss very little of what happens in any aspect of life. The dynamic that is created on your team, their posture, and their performance, will all belong to you in the long run of your coaching responsibility. I would dare say that many coaches choose not to shoulder the perceived burden of taking over a failing program. But the risks will diminish and the results of your efforts will be enjoyed, many times over, as you begin building a successful program from the ground up.

Much of the sweetness and the richness of your wrestler's individual and team accomplishments will be heightened and enhanced because of the depth and degree of what you must overcome in this type of demanding environment. The care and expertise that you will provide for them during the efforts it will take to build a winning tradition, or to resurrect what had become a losing program, will be the kind of experience that will change your life. It will affirm your appreciation for the benefits of hard work and it will enhance your own sense of well-being, and deservedly so.

The sacrifices you will make will not go unnoticed by any one wrestler on your team. Some will not acknowledge that fact until many years later. They will not all necessarily appear to like you during all phases of the journey. But all will eventually respect you. It may not be until you get a phone call from the dance floor of their 15th year class reunion where three of your state champions and place winners are discussing what was really important to them, and they just want you to know what you've done for their lives.

Tyler Brock, 2x State qualifier and place winner who made the phone call along with Rob Atkinson and Brandon Cartee, West Henderson High School coached by Darrell McDowell.

Or, they may start to call you about generating a wrestling reunion to celebrate all the great teams from past successes. They will want to talk about what they have begun to remember as the best times of their lives. They will want to re-live the wins and talk about what they're doing and why they have become successful, usually expressing that much of it, is due in great part, to the attitudes and ambitions that were galvanized because of their participation on your team and in the sport of wrestling.

16

Program Essentials

I *was married on December 17, 1983. If you coaches will notice, this is right in the heart of wrestling season. I had prescribed this important affair on the day I received the opportunity to become the new wrestling coach at Madison/Mayodan High School.*

To be more specific about how I got to the altar, four months before the big day at the Baptist Church in Naples, NC, I was out in the pasture at Red Top Farm in Big Willow pulling rusty nails out of an old barn with a crow bar when my dad came down and told me that I had received a phone call from the placement office at ASU about a teaching job somewhere near Greensboro, NC that might include football and wrestling. It was August 13th and I had just completed my last semester in college at Appalachian State. The summer semester I had just finished was needed to catch up a few credits I had lost when I transferred from Pembroke State University in the middle of my freshmen year. This scenario put me into the teaching market late in the game. So this was not a time for me to be picky about a chance to interview.

It was hot and I was nasty and sweaty. I left the work I was doing at the farm early and called to get the number I needed about the teaching position. I had never heard of Western Rockingham City Schools at the time. But I certainly was interested, especially considering the fact that I had no alternative. I made a phone call to the Central Office in Madison where I was put on a speaker phone with Jeter Taylor who was the Principal. Also present were the personnel director and the assistant superintendent for the district. They asked me a few questions about what I might be able to offer them in terms of experience and then they asked me if I could come down the next day for an interview. When I said yes, he said, "Can you come down today." It was one p.m. in the afternoon by then and it was about a four hour drive to Rockingham County. And I had no idea where I was going. But I said yes anyway.

I then thought about how hot it was and my old green 1970 Camaro had no air conditioning, so I called my girlfriend, Lisa Brevard, another Hendersonville native, and asked her if I could borrow her car for the trip. We had been dating for two years and she said yes. At that point, I told her that I felt like I might get the job. And then, out of the blue, I asked her if she would marry me. She said "Wherever you're going, I'm going too." This was turning out to be a very big day.

It seemed like an eternity on the trip and I kept thinking, "How can I still be in North Carolina?" as I headed toward the Virginia state line. I missed the first turn in Rockingham County at the Wentworth/Madison exit, so I got off at the next one down, where I made a phone call from some go-cart track. It was about five-thirty p.m. by then and the administrators were still waiting at the Central Office for my arrival. When I finally got there, I went in and sat down in my peach colored polo shirt and gray coaching pants. Before you get too critical, it was all I had at the time and I didn't have a wife to tell me any different.

Jeter Taylor, the principal, began to ask me questions about my philosophies on instruction and coaching. He followed a bit of a protocol for a few minutes and then they all shut up while I began to profess all that I truly believed about the importance of education, wrestling, football and a number of other convictions that I had about life at the ripe old age of twenty-two years. I figured I needed to tell it like it was in that situation. If I didn't get the job, I didn't even know where I was anyway. And I figured I would eventually find my way back to the mountains again.

At the end of the interview Jeter Taylor said, "I've got to tell you son, you have missed your calling, you should have been either a preacher or a used car salesman, and I'm not sure which one would have been better." Then they asked me to step outside their office to the secretary's desk in the lobby and about ten minutes later they opened the door and said, "We would like to offer you a contract." I had never seen the school or the town and I said, "Give it here. I'll sign it!"

Anyway, I got a wife, a job, a varsity football coaching position, and became a head wrestling coach all in one day. I spent the week I should have been on a honeymoon that year getting ready to wrestle Rockingham County High School during that December and that is really the only regret I've had about any of it. Thankfully, after twenty three years and three children, I still have this patient and understanding wife. And she is much of the reason I have had any of the success I've enjoyed over the years.

Program essentials are not always about techniques, strategies and trophies. They're about commitment, dedication, growth and family.

⊙⊙⊙

As you begin to construct the plan for your program, there are a few basic perspectives and philosophies that should help guide your vision for laying the kind of groundwork that will ensure your success. The most important elements of consideration include family, academics, and then wrestling.

Family Portrait of the McDowell Family. Left to right: Cameron, Lisa, Candice, Darrell and Christin. Photo provided by Bill Keller of Expression's Photography in Flat Rock, NC.

For those of you that are just getting started as new coaches, be very careful to emphasize the first two that I have mentioned to a degree that will provide a solid foundation for you to build your program. Even outstanding technicians and former wrestlers aspiring to becoming coaches out there will have difficulty sustaining the results they expect if they take a one-dimensional approach to working with the teenagers that will be in their charge.

As you begin to have meetings with your team, and with your athlete's parents, you will need to have a visible and understandable vision, and a strong belief in the level of structure that you are about to demand. If you appear to falter with your efforts to maintain the continuity of your ideas, or digress from the announced framework of what you tell them will be expected, you risk the credibility and integrity of your program. It will be much easier to enforce expectations and be enthusiastic about moving forward with your plan for success if you have confidence and a clear vision for what you want. The principles that you choose to believe in, and the direction that you attempt to sell to your program, should be noble and substantial. Your expectations should reflect an ambitious process that has value and clear potential for ensuring positive change in the lives of your wrestlers.

Parents need to feel that you have an interest in their child that goes beyond the boundaries of the wrestling arena. For those of you that are professional educators, this should not be a difficult aspiration for you. If you have made a decision at some point in your life to spend a career working with children, then I would presume that your passion for the coaching responsibility, though very important to some of us, is a secondary motivation as to why you are working in education.

As you begin to develop your schedules for matches and contests, you will need to consider how you are going to ensure at least a minimal amount of time for your athletes to spend during the Christmas Holidays with their parents. There will be many opportunities around this time of year for you to engage your athletes in intensive Invitational, or Christmas tournaments that will be important for you to consider as you attempt to prepare your athletes for the rest of the season. But, you may want to consider either attending one on the front end, or the back end of the holiday rather than ignoring a chance for your kids to take a short time-out with the people that are most important in their lives. And, you need to tell the parents what you are doing, and why you are going to do it at the introductory meeting, at the beginning of the season. They will appreciate your efforts, and most will plan accordingly. Because of your consideration for what is most important for their family, you will gain a respected advantage with these same parents when they have to face the many other sacrifices you will ask of them as you proceed toward the State Tournament.

Cameron McDowell checking out his "First pair of Wrestling Shoes" at Christmas.

Another detail of consideration for parents in your program can be demonstrated at the last home match of the regular season. For the troubles and the time they have forfeited to help ensure the success of the wrestling program, it will serve you well to prepare a senior night to recognize and celebrate, not only the dedication and commitment of your senior wrestlers, managers, film staff, and statisticians, but also to honor the contributions and sacrifices that are made by the wrestling parents.

Parent night normally consists of a pre-match ceremony for the public that are in attendance at the last home match that identifies the career accomplishments of your senior wrestlers, equips the senior mothers with a rose, or a corsage, and to act on a last chance to highlight the senior fathers with a handshake of appreciation for their participation in the program. This ritual needs to be established as a tradition, an instrument of your continued effort to create a positive culture, and to reinforce the fraternal order of your wrestling program.

17

Academics

I'm probably either the worst or the best person to discuss *the academics of wrestling. In the early days I was no scholar. I had no idea that I might attempt to go to college until my junior year at West Henderson High School. I had never been in a college prep course before that time. And I must admit that my grade point average wasn't anything to brag about to that point in my coursework. But I was beginning to realize, because of what I had begun to accomplish in athletics, wrestling in particular, that I was able to achieve just about anything if I set goals and put my mind to it. I began taking a challenging English course with a superior teacher named Mary Ellen O'shields, who sold me on the merits of Emerson and Thoreau, and I had great success in an advanced Biology course. I guess skinning all those squirrels in my youth had a positive affect on naming the parts of the formaldehyde cats we had in the labs. As my confidence began to grow, I decided to go to the school guidance office and ask for some help.*

I remember walking in the administrative building at lunch one day and asking to speak to a counselor. There were certain places in the school, like the gym, or the auditorium where I guess I could have been perceived as a little cocky or at least confident at times, but the guidance office was not one of these places. I was fairly reserved in that environment.

I was looking at some of the university brochures when Mary Ruth Heil, the head counselor at West, attempted to address my request. She had been there forever and at that time she probably looked to be in her early sixties. She had gray hair, a proper posture, and a professional approach with her bedside manner. She asked how she might be able to help and I just stated that I thought I might want to go to college. Apparently she had already seen my transcripts from years' past. Because the next question out of her mouth was, "Well Darrell, have you considered joining the military?" I said, "No mam, I'm really interested in trying to wrestle in college." And she said, "Well have you thought about a community college."

Ms. Heil was a sweet lady and I am sure she treated me just like she would have treated anyone else. But she had no way of knowing what I knew about me, or at least what I was beginning to learn. The sport of wrestling could not change who I had been as a student but it would definitely change who I would become. The work ethic, the goal setting, and the improved confidence that I found on the mat was transferred firmly toward the books and the classroom. Ms. Heil had no way to predict that I would graduate from college with a 3.2 GPA, gain a Masters Degree with a 3.6, and sit on 4.0 in a Doctoral Program.

Another area that can cripple your potential success lies in the failure to address the academic status of each of your athletes. Do not allow this to be a secondary consideration. Many otherwise excellent teams have been struck down by this avoidable problem. Some schools have more trouble than others with this potential calamity. Academics can be affected by the overall climate of expectations that is set by the administration or by the coaches. If your school doesn't have a tutoring program in place that you can enroll your deficient wrestlers in at the beginning of the season, then you will need to set up your own process for helping meet the academic needs of your wrestlers.

The first thing you should do is to insist on a level of academic performance that rivals that of your expectations for them on the mat. Just as you need to ask them to review their athletic goals with you, related to succeeding in the sport, there should be an expectation, especially with the critical cases, that wrestlers review their mid-terms and report cards with you with the same regularity. This not only gives you a chance to check on their need for help, but it also gives you an opportunity to praise them for their improved academic efforts, which will often help motivate them to work toward a positive process with their grades.

There are few things in sports that are more heartbreaking than when an exceptionally talented or hard working athlete is ejected from his dreams because he fails to meet academic standards for participation. This unfortunate, and most of the time, unnecessary disaster, can sometimes lead to the complete destruction of both athletic and academic hopes. It can also destroy a team's dream of championship success whether it is a conference, regional, dual team, or individual tournament competition.

Wrestling coaches sometimes have to learn the hard way to find ways to help their wrestlers academically. Often developing positive relationships with teachers and administrators in the school will be helpful with your efforts to stay informed and stay on top of this issue. Fortunately, once your program is fully established, the expectation for successful performance in everything you do will begin to enhance the academic success of most of your wrestlers. Most will be individually driven to stay eligible. And a fair percentage will begin to assert their academic gains toward receiving honor student recognitions.

18

Extra Help: Statisticians, Managers, Camera People and Score Keepers

As your program begins to take hold in the school environment, you will begin to recognize that you have to delegate some of the technical and logistical operations to others. I found that most of the best and most reliable candidates for these jobs were actually students. They were people who had the time, and were searching for chances to assume responsibility and to be recognized for their efforts. They were allowed to mature as they learned what they needed to know to become successful in the program.

After several years of seeing the benefits of growing my own managers, statisticians and film crews, I began to realize that they were just as proud, just as loyal, and in a less intensive and physical way, just as dedicated to our efforts to ensure the success of our wrestling program as anyone else on the team.

What I also found out was that many of these "extra hands" would go on to do the same jobs at the collegiate level and sometimes make an even greater contribution at the next level. They were just as informed about expectations, rules, and regulations, as the wrestling competitors, and more attentive to the details and logistical elements of the program that the rest of us would not have time to put under the microscope. Many of these people have gone forward as adults, like the wrestlers, and attributed much of their collegiate and career successes to what they had learned about work, and winning, during their association with the wrestling program.

Many of them were males. But a large number of them were females who endured the intensive, and sometimes volatile, environment that was created in, and around practices, matches and tournaments. Many of these young people came out of that situation with a passion, and a deep understanding of the importance of personal vision and a plan for success. Many times during their efforts with the team, they were able to offer suggestions and contribute extra time to the program that made significant differences in the decisions that were made, and in the actions that were taken, toward the overall success of our wrestling team.

One great example of one of these individuals was Jennifer Adams. When I coached at West Henderson High School, she spent three years in the program. She knew everything that you could possibly know about what I wanted for the team. She and several like her took care of a lot of the details at matches and tournaments that allowed me to focus on coaching the kids rather than dealing with so much of the clerical and organizational responsibilities. Jennifer went on to work for Coach Mance at Appalachian State University in a similar capacity while she was in college. She is still often involved with the middle and high school tournaments that are organized in Henderson County, North

Carolina, where she now works as a Media Coordinator for Flat Rock Middle School.

Jennifer Adams Northrup, score keeper and Manager at West Henderson High. Coach, Darrell McDowell and at Appalachian State University, Coach Paul Mance.

Most of the support-people in the program became very confident about offering suggestions about logistical operations with little fear about the fact that I would often say "no." Even with this non-competitive group of team members, fear was not a respected element of who they were becoming or an acceptable part of their way of thinking. Most grew to understand the necessity and the expectation of sacrifice, and the commitment to the greater good of the program goals.

Many of these young people have gone on to become teachers, law enforcement officers and other respected professionals. Most are candid about the benefits they have gained from the wrestling environment. As a wrestling coach you will, at times, need to solicit the help of other adults to ensure the success of your program. But, do not underestimate the importance to your program of the non-wrestling students who are dedicated and committed to the team. And maybe, even more important do not miss the chance to change their lives in a way that will ensure their adult success. As with the wrestlers, you will be rewarded as a coach, with a feeling of great pride and appreciation for their efforts and their on-going accomplishments.

There is one particular support person that has become a very recognizable figure in the Wrestling World during his many years of service. Bob Mauldin spent several years as a manager and a scorekeeper for "Red" Watkins and Joe Edminston, at Appalachian State University, before he became the founder and editor of the very popular and heavily circulated wrestling publication entitled the "Mat News." Bob's contribution to the children in the Kannapolis, NC area as a school administrator, and his gifts of recognition to the wrestling athletes and coaches in the sport that he loves, has been phenomenal. This sport often creates a contagious level of enthusiasm among it participants that ensures our involvement in the game for a lifetime. Bob was recently inducted and recognized in the "National Wrestling Hall of Fame" in Stillwater, Oklahoma with a "Lifetime Service Award."

Bob Mauldin, Editor of the NC "Mat News" with his "trademark hat."

19

Gender

In recent years, a new point of interest and controversy has come with the addition of female athletes who have made the decision to participate in wrestling. There are probably far more opinions on the appropriateness of this phenomenon than there are actual female participants in the sport to this point. I am a former coach with a daughter that once aspired to becoming a wrestler, due in part because of her association with an exceptional program and a daddy who values the benefits of this game to the greatest degree.

I have grappled with the many possibilities related to the gender issue as a coach and a father. I must admit that in my own daughter's situation, as the parents of a female child who wanted to compete in wrestling, we declined to allow her participation in the sport until it had gained enough momentum to provide a competitive pool of girls that were motivated to compete in the amateur clubs, and in the organized and sanctioned female tournaments that are sponsored by some of the national wrestling organizations.

Whether or not that was an appropriate, or productive, way to contend with her situation, I guess, I will really never know. In her late high school years, my daughter did compete, in an all-girls nationally advertised tournament in Atlanta, Georgia and she was very competitive. Honestly, our only problem with the issue, as parents, was really the idea of her participation in matches against boys. And some of our reasoning may not be what you might expect. Of course like any red blooded father, the idea of your daughter spending six minutes on the mat with a male competitor, who is required to put his hands on who knows where, even in a genuine effort to survive the potential pummeling he might sustain at the hands of my four feet, 11 inch, blue eyed angel, just cripple my perception about what I really do think is wonderful about the female participation in this incredible sport.

Candice McDowell, on the left at a "Strong and Courageous" Club Practice preparing for a nationally advertised Female Tournament in Atlanta, GA. Photo courtesy of Hendersonville North Carolina "Times News", Photographer: Chris Clevenger/Times-News.

There are tremendous opportunities for girls to improve their skill levels with increased mat time, and the potential exists for them to gain high levels of genuinely competitive experience by engaging with boys that could act as successful drilling partners. As would have been the case with my own daughter, the difficulty may lie in the girl's efforts to find opportunities where the boys are willing to set aside the time to practice with females. Although, I am sure there do already exist practice situations where this happens regularly, I would think that the jury is probably still out, with regard to large-scale co-ed participation as a common occurrence.

I truly believe that females deserve the same opportunity to compete in the sport and to enjoy the tremendous benefits that I have discussed here-to-fore in amateur wrestling. And I am often fascinated by, and truly respectful of, the levels of skill that are being gained at an exponential rate among the female competitors.

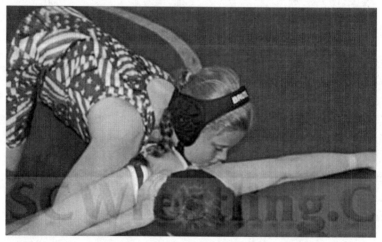

Isabella Leftwich attempts to turn a male opponent to his back. Photo provided by John Carpenter.

Female amateur wrestling, especially at the club and youth levels, is well on its way to being a legitimate and a recognized part of the sports world. But in fairness, after having boys and girls in my own family that have attempted to participate in wrestling, both my wife and I have had some real concern about what it really means for a young man who may actually have to endure a physical pounding by a female competitor, and what that may mean for that individual from a personal and cultural perspective. As a parent, I have had to contend with a daughter that wanted to a wrestle, and a son who has had to compete in the sport against girls.

I must also admit that I have had the opportunity on several occasions to coach against female competitors, even at the high school level. I always suggest to the male team member that I am sending him on the mat to approach the match with same level of competitive vigor that he would be expected to produce against a male opponent. But I have seen coaches that refuse to send their male competitor onto the mat in that situation. Or there are some coaches that suggest that the male athlete take it easy on the female. None of these scenarios are good for either the male or the female athlete. I must also admit that there is a part of me that understands the potential dilemma these young men may be facing from a public perspective, and the confusion that comes with regard to how men are raised to treat women.

In no way do I misunderstand the motivation of the female athletes. And, I have a tremendous respect for a female wrestler that has the ambition and the fearless attitude that inspires her to enter into the kind of non-traditional and high-risk environment that awaits her in such an intensive and demanding arena of competition. There are clearly, at this time, few options for the girls to compete in the sport outside of agreeing to wrestle boys at the scholastic level of amateur competition in most states in America. So, in no way am I opposed to, or even negatively predisposed with my feelings about a female wrestler's plight to improve her skills, and her chance to find success in the male wrestling arena. But, there are still some issues that need to be considered and clarified.

In more detail, the problem that can arise from this new co-ed form of competition can sometimes lie in the path of the male competitor. Unfortunately, when a male competitor is seeded in a bracket with a female wrestler it can become a lose-lose proposition. If the male competitor is superior to the female wrestler and delivers an aggressive, or punishing level of performance in his effort to win, he will likely be criticized by the general public for his precision, and his intensive efforts. Clearly, this is no fault of his, or of the female opponent. In normal circumstances, this sport rewards toughness and tenacity. This scenario can be in conflict with typical cultural and sociological expectations.

This perplexing issue is probably related to, and affected by, everything most young boys since their time of birth, have been taught about how they are suppose to treat a woman, and rightly so. This conflicting interaction of competition and psychological alienation, or at least inhibition, could potentially distort the expected performance by the male competitor. One might argue that a truly disciplined and pure athlete would find a way to overcome any obstacle he has to face on the mat. But this issue has less to do with athleticism and more to do with what may be expected by his coach, his parents, or what he believes the world may think of his performance, whether it is in victory or defeat.

Isabella Leftwich fights hard off her back in a coed match. Isabella is from the state of South Carolina. Photo provided by John Carpenter.

On the other hand, although there are exceptions, most female athletes in their final stages of development lack the physical prowess and physiological maturation that eventually occurs in the male wrestlers. There are many talented women that are probably capable of defeating a large percentage of the men in the average male population in this country at their particular weight classes. And, what may be far worse for the male competitor is the realistic potential, especially in the lower levels of competition such as elementary, middle, and in some high school matches, when the male wrestler suffers a loss at the hands of the female opponent. There are some female wrestlers that defeat many male athletes on a regular basis.

The results of this phenomenon, again culturally inspired, may create any number of social consequences for the boy that loses to the girl. What this young man may endure can be very difficult to defend or recover from because of the pervasive preconceived ideas and expectations related to common beliefs and cultural expectations that are held about girls and boys in general. He will very likely pay an even greater price for losing the match than he might have suffered had he won the match. Because in a coed competition, it would be a fair estimate to say that ninety percent of the wrestling fans in the arena, and most of his friends at school, will probably expect him to succeed against a girl, no matter how good she may be.

The loudest and most intensive complaints that I have heard at these contests are usually initiated by the women, especially the mothers of the young men, my wife included, who are faced with the reality that there son may have to endure the difficulties that the world has in store for the boy, whether it's because he is brutal with his tactics against the girl or if he has to suffer the severe consequences of losing against a female opponent. Often these mothers have worked very hard to see that their young sons are raised to respect and care about the women in their life so that they grow up to be exceptional husbands and fathers.

In theory, this sport provides the pure potential for any wrestler to beat another opponent on any given day. The introduction of women to the wrestling mat appears to have brought with it an entanglement of issues that will surely iron themselves out as we progress with the new realities that are on the horizon for the sport.

Ashley Carver and Brittany Delgado compete in a female wrestling match. Both girls are competitive athletes from the Up-state South Carolina Area. Photo provided by John Carpenter.

We may be evolving toward a positive and natural transition of women taking advantage of the opportunities to get the clearly documented benefits of what wrestling has to offer all participants in the game. In the birth of all new things there is usually an element of suffering and criticism. These female athletes are pioneers in their own right, trying to find their passion in a unique set of dynamics that were not contoured, or developed, to meet their particular needs or angle of concerns. The issues and perceptions that have been raised in this material are real and should be at least considered as women are integrated in a mainstream effort to include them as a legitimate part of the game. Girl's athletics such as basketball, softball and volleyball are drawing impressive crowds all over the country. I am comfortable that this sport given time and opportunity will gain the momentum needed to ensure a strong level of participation, acceptance and success for women wrestlers.

Christin McDowell swinging the bat at her Youth Softball game in Henderson County, North Carolina.

Sarah McMann

Sarah McMann in Greece. She competed in the Female Freestyle Wrestling Competition during the 2004 Olympic Games. Sarah secured a silver medal in her first Olympic Games as a result of her hard fought efforts. Photograph provided by Tim Hutchins, Head Wrestling Coach at McDowell High School in Marion, North Carolina.

The entry of female wrestlers into the Olympics during the 2004 Games in Greece has given them the publicity and a legitimacy that has been felt all over the country.

Having been a coach and a school administrator in the Carolinas, and still working with the wrestlers in a club organization in this area, I was able to observe the excitement that our kids felt about the female competition that took place in Greece. Many of our wrestlers and coaches had a strong interest in following the silver medal performance of Sarah McMann in the Olympic Freestyle Competition.

Sarah McMann was one of the first competitive female scholastic wrestlers in North Carolina. She was a member of an otherwise all male team where she wrestled for Coach Tim Hutchins in the starting line-up at McDowell High School in the Western part of the state. Coach Hutchins has had continued growth and success in the Wrestling program at McDowell High School for the last seventeen years. The school is located about an hour down the mountain from Boone in a small town called Marion, in McDowell County.

During the time that Sarah went to high school in North Carolina, she also participated with the Strong and Courageous Amateur Wrestling Club for a period of time. The club, coached by Norman Osteen, is now located in the Asheville/Hendersonville area of the state. Club members, both male and female, anxiously awaited the results to come in from Sarah's performance in the Olympics Games. Her silver medal performance generated a lot of interest and enthusiasm among all wrestlers in the area on the part of both girls and boys. This type of exposure definitely helps to increase the level of participation and interest by females in the country and opens many doors for helping female amateur wrestling to get a foothold toward becoming a mainstream sport.

Sarah McMann with her hand raised in air after a victory in the 2004 Olympic Games in Greece. Photograph provided by Tim Hutchins, Head Wrestling Coach at McDowell High School in Marion, NC.

Amateur wrestling competition for females is clearly well on its way to having a successful position in the future of this game. The outstanding efforts on behalf of motivated wrestlers, coaches and parents to ensure opportunities for these young women will undoubtedly create avenues of growth and success that will have beneficial and long-lasting effects. Every child, whether they are male or female certainly deserves a chance to gain the clear benefits associated with spending quality time on the mat, and a chance to work and communicate with the exceptional people that are involved in the sport.

Sarah McMann represents much of what is exciting and respected about the new opportunities that exist in Amateur Wrestling for female athletes. Her successful performance in Greece, along with the recent accomplishments of several other elite female wrestlers will help pave the way for volumes of young girls to be accepted in this game, and it should help to open the door to the hopes and the dreams of many more.

20

The Spiritual Choice

*E*verywhere I have ever coached wrestling I have also coached football. When I went to West Henderson I was notified about the position because the school needed a varsity line coach as well as a varsity head wrestling coach. When I left my position as a head wrestling and varsity football coach at Madison/Mayodan High School I was already having a successful coaching career. But I left to come back to my home in the mountains. I was also intrigued by the idea of coaching football under head coach Carroll Wright at West. He had come into the West High community and turned the football program around. He had two consecutive years of undefeated seasons with the Falcons. I learned a great deal about a lot of things during the two years I spent coaching in his football program.

One thing I will never forget was something he said during a discussion we were having about religion and football. Like wrestling, football is a very emotional and physical contest. On game day you could hardly speak to the man. Coach Wright is one of the most intense people I have ever met. He was in his late fifties when I worked for him and on Fridays he might as well have had on a helmet and shoulder *pads. He truly believed that he was preparing for war. He always had a devotional before each game. He usually had a community minister or a team chaplain who would deliver an inspirational message or a positive story that might move his group of players closer to a chance to enter the battlefield on Friday night with a greater sense of hope and confidence.*

At one point during our season he said he was getting concerned about the pre-game message. He was worried that it was getting a little mellow. As he discussed this issue with the coaching staff he was fairly graphic about what he wanted. As he wrestled with this concern, he became truly emotional about what needed to happen. He didn't want to hurt our speaker's feelings but he began thinking out loud and we all actually began to grin about his despair when he said, "Come on. These meek and mild, love your brother speeches are killing us. We just need somebody to tell it like it is. Give us something about Samson breaking off them ropes and taking the jawbone of an ass and slaying a thousand men." We all ended up breaking into a full blown laugh about his graphic description about what we needed to help motivate our players. And he finally joined us in the fun we were having with his sense of despair. But he was very sincere about what he thought he needed to do to inspire his players.

I too believe there is great opportunity for many athletes that look to their faith and their religious leaders for support and comfort. By the way, that scripture does actually exist in the Bible in Judges 15:9-17. I checked it out to make sure he knew what he was talking about.

Rulon Gardner was a 2000 Olympic Champion in Greco-Roman Wrestling and Dremiel Byers, in the Army singlet, is one of the current top ranked Greco-Roman Heavyweight competitors in the World. Dremiel wrestled for Steve Moffitt at Kings Mountain High School in Kings Mountain, North Carolina, only a short drive from Charlotte, North Carolina. He was also a North Carolina State Champion in 1993. These two giants in the sport were caught on film kneeling together in prayer at the Olympic Trials in Indianapolis, prior to the 2004 Olympics Games in Greece. Photograph provided by Tom Carter, Head Wrestling Coach at Erwin High School near Asheville, NC.

Since writing this book is not a school sponsored activity, I'm assuming that I am not governed by a Circuit Court somewhere that restricts me from talking about my version of the spiritual side of the wrestling game. It is not my desire to preach to any of you. But to ignore such a substantial element of the wrestling game, for so many of its participants, would be a ridiculous shortfall on behalf of a high percentage of tremendously successful competitors.

Many individual competitors proclaim to sustain high levels of enhanced performance in the sport and feel free to enter the matches with a heightened sense of confidence, and a greater sense of personal safety for both the wrestler, and his opponent, due to a convicted, and ensured, personal association with a higher power.

Religious convictions are displayed and proclaimed as an enhancement and a necessary function by many wrestlers across the country. Like other sports, each competitor in wrestling has to find his own path to survival and success. Although the present Circuit Court directives prohibit adult sponsors from leading prayers in school sponsored activities, you will often find many individuals in the amateur wrestling world that secure great hope and a profound sense of confidence in their own brand of communication with their God. Often many teams will recite the Lord's Prayer prior to the initiation of the first match at every competition. This ritual is legal as long as it is generated and led by a student leader and must include optional participation. No one should be made to feel as if they are a part of a captive audience in a school-sponsored event.

The nature of this particular game demands a high level of self-reflection. The potential for physical exhaustion, injury, emotional excess and public failure, create conditions that mesh well with the benefits offered by the religious experience.

The sheer isolation of the contest and massiveness of the individual challenge that often sets into the mind of each competitor, after pulling up the last strap on the wrestling singlet, and popping the snap on the head gear, creates the need to find a sense of peace and confidence. Individually initiated pre-match prayers are a commonly identified occurrence in the routines of many of the competitors at every level of the Amateur Wrestling World. I will reiterate that no one should be required to participate in this ritual. And no restriction should be imposed on any one individual, or group or arena of followers that depend on this additional sense of hope and motivation, and the sense of empowerment they seek from their God.

Strong and Courageous Club wrestlers and coaches close practice with a team prayer on the mat. The prayer was led on that night by James Shurt, a former NC State Champ from North Henderson High School.

Most wrestlers, in their faith, ask not for pins, wins, or championships, but for the strength to take advantage of their God-given talents, and to be able to utilize what they have learned about life and about the sport of wrestling. They ask for the power to face the inevitable adversity that will appear on the mat with a welcoming spirit, to embrace the challenge that lies ahead without the fear, or doubt, that can accompany those who have less accessibility to the eternal resources that are afforded to them by their faith. They ask for God's presence during their physical, mental, and emotional efforts on the mat. And, most ask to be free of all burdens and obstacles that might hinder their ultimate success, contribute to their failure, or affect the safety of either competitor. But, the sum of all pre-match prayers usually asks that the Lord's will be done.

Not only do individuals and various teams regularly engage in prayer as part of their traditional wrestling experience, but there are also a number of clubs and teams that profess to be founded as "faith-based" organizations. Two of my own children, one male, and one female, have been members of Coach Norman Osteen's "Strong and Courageous" Club Wrestling Organization for several years. His club is a faith-based organization that combines opportunities for young people from both North and South Carolina.

Coach Norman Osteen, Head Coach and Club Organizer for "Strong and Courageous" works with Mitchell Langford and Aaron Owensby at a Club practice.

Coach Osteen's efforts and philosophies help young wrestlers in the Western part of the both states to gain excellent weekly wrestling instruction, matches and drilled mat time, transportation to tournaments, and optional exposure to participation in religious devotionals that are constructed in a religious framework that is relative to the wrestling environment. There is a very strong element of parental participation in both the competition structure, and in the faith-based operations of the club.

Strong and Courageous team picture 2005.

As a former high school coach and principal, I am keenly aware of the rules and regulations of the separation and the entanglement of church and state. And, I am respectful of the need to adhere to the legal framework of this issue. But, I have had many occasions, as a leader or a guest speaker, to discuss my faith in an appropriate arena such as the Fellowship of Christian Athlete's meetings and at Club Wrestling Devotionals. And, there is one particular passage in the book of Ephesians that has helped provide great comfort and a tremendous inspiration and motivation to my own success as a competitor, as a coach, and in my personal life, that I would re-miss not to mention.

If you have an interest in finding a tool that can be instrumental in helping you to find strength and give guidance to helping prepare for a wrestling match, or to engage in other significant challenges, the Holy Bible is a good place to start. There is one particular passage in the King James Version of the Holy Bible that can prepare you to face the obstacles in your path.

This section of the written word offers tremendous guidance as you pursue your goals as a wrestler, or as a coach, or when you just need a reminder of the eternal resource that exists for those of us who believe in God. The passage is entitled "The Armor of God." And, like the lessons that are learned on the mat, and in your wrestling programs, the words in this scripture can be readily transferred and translated to other situations and circumstances that are orchestrated on the mat, and in everyday life.

Ephesians, 6:10-20 King James Version:
Armor of God

10 Finally, my brethren, be strong in the Lord, and in the power of his might. 11 Put on the whole armor of God, that ye may be able to stand against the wiles of the devil. 12 For we wrestle not against flesh and blood, but against principalities, against powers, against the rulers of the darkness of this world, against spiritual wickedness in high places.
13 Wherefore take unto you the whole armor of God that ye may be able to withstand in the evil day, and having done

all, to stand. 14 Stand therefore, having your loins girt about with truth, and having on the breastplate of righteousness; 15 and your feet shod with the preparation of the gospel of peace; 16 above all, taking the shield of faith, wherewith ye shall be able to quench all the fiery darts of the wicked. 17 And take the helmet of salvation, and the sword of the Spirit, which is the word of God: 18 praying always with all prayer and supplication for all saints; 19 and for me, that utterance may be given to me, that I may open my mouth boldly, to make known the mystery of the gospel, 20 for which I am an ambassador in bonds; that therein I may speak boldly, as I ought to speak.

This set of principles is clearly written to offer the confidence and composure needed to engage in a conflict against an outside evil or spiritual entity. But the tone and the metaphoric analogies described in the scripture inspire thoughts of exceptional preparation and a reinforced confidence about entering into any arena with a prepared sense of freedom, and a well-equipped sense of ambition for entering into the heat of competition.

This particular piece of scripture was obviously written to surpass any potential needs that we might have to face in a mere wrestling match. But, it also allows us to be mindful of the expansive spiritual resources that are available to all of us, as we proceed with the difficult tasks that we have to endure. I would challenge all wrestlers, coaches, and parents to take the chance to reflect on this motivational piece of historical and religious literature. It can provide a profound sense of hope in almost any situation, and it has powerful implications for helping us to face the daily challenges in our lives.

Granted, the Carolina area is located in the "Bible Belt." And, the improved quality and levels of increased participation in wrestling are definitely in the growth mode, when compared with some of the overall skill levels and traditions that have evolved in states like Pennsylvania or Ohio, and in areas of the northeast, and Midwestern states, where the sport has already become well established over the years. But the evolution of the clubs, traveling teams, and organized practice opportunities are beginning to offer a great benefit for improving the performances of the future high school and college wrestlers in this area of the country.

Matt Baynard, Strong and Courageous Club Wrestler controls the match.

The Strong and Courageous Club that was previously mentioned is located in the western part of the Carolinas, and it fits well with the wrestling needs and the religious tone for this area. Coach Osteen's organization provides many opportunities to help keep kids off the street and on the mat. His program provides the adult instruction, individual guidance, and the transportation needed to get some of these kids to competitive events that they would not have otherwise been able to attend. Many of the competitions that are included on his list of scheduled events are national tournaments, and they are balanced with opportunities to participate in a variety of other competitive regional and local events.

Strong and Courageous Club Members, photographed after competing at Lakota High School in an Ohio, USA Tournament near Cincinnati, in the spring of 2005.

21

Taking the High Road

*I*have been very lucky during my years as a wrestling coach to have worked with some very professional and considerate basketball coaches in this great basketball state of North Carolina. Danny Anderson, who was the head boys coach for the varsity team at Madison/Mayodan, was a great friend both professionally and socially. He is now the head coach at West Caldwell High School in the Mountains. We always worked well together on scheduling practices and matches and tried to be considerate of each others needs. When I went to Madison the principal had allowed me to tear out a space under the cafeteria to assemble a semi-effective place to practice and we made out pretty well in the facility.

When I arrived at West Henderson the practice situation was even worse. We had to roll up mats everyday and we often did our running in the auditorium, which was on a slight grade, forcing us to run up and then down as we circled through the facility. It was far from perfect. But when I set the pace for our success, I had told the kids that if we have to practice in the bed of a pickup truck or in the school yard we were going to find success and we did.

While I was at West Henderson a new basketball coach by the name of Rick Wood showed up on the scene with a strong history of winning games in the mountains. I had gotten to know him during two-a-days in a football camp when I had roomed with him at North Greenville College. In the early days of his career at West he had agreed to help coach the J.V. football team in an arrangement that would allow him to become the new varsity boys' coach at the school. He was a nice Christian man. I remember the collection of religious hymns he played while we were rooming together at the football camp. He was organized and professional with his approach to spawning the same kind of success that I was beginning to enjoy in the wrestling program.

A year went by and I had attempted to help Rick in any way that I could to ensure his success with the basketball situation. And then one day after practice Coach Wood brought his J.V. Coach Jim Hyatt and asked if they might speak to me about an issue they had with a conflict. And could I step in the gym office for a moment? I should have known something was up when I saw Coach Hyatt attached to the process. He was a very good friend of mine. We had been coaching football together for a long time before Rick showed up as the head basketball coach.

Rick said that he was afraid we had a little problem. He went on to say that he noticed on my wrestling schedule that I had a varsity match on a night that he had decided to have a home basketball scrimmage. He then asked me what I thought I could I do about this problem? It was after a tough practice. My kids had just carried mats from the cafeteria lobby so that he could practice in the gym. I probably could have been a little more diplomatic with my response, but I said, "Rick the honeymoon is over. I will do anything I can to help you with your program, but not at the expense of mine." I'm afraid I was a little more abrupt with my response than I probably should have been. Even Jim, my good friend, the J.V. coach looked a little shocked at my response. But at that point it was time to stand up for my kids and my program. I had begun to feel the tide of the basketball dominance rising to a level of interference on that day that forced me to firm up my position by reminding him of the significance of the wrestling program. The schedule stayed as I had made it that year and we worked well together at all times following that meeting.

Rick has had tremendous success as the basketball coach in the years since he arrived at West and I truly respect the kind of man he is. Take the high road if you can. But have the courage to ensure the success and the integrity that your wrestlers deserve. Just try to do it in a professional manner.

Much of this book was inspired by a burning desire to ensure wrestling's place in the overall hierarchy of the sports world. Unfortunately, it is an exceptional, but somewhat misunderstood, and under-utilized opportunity for many young people. Participation in this game could help ensure great numbers of youths with a well-deserved sense of self-worth, and a better chance to get a jump-start on a successful way of life. But some would say that the amateur wrestling world woke up one day and found ourselves to be a little bit of a "stepchild" when compared to the levels of participation and popularity enjoyed by some of the other major sports. I understand the relative comparison, but I believe that we are sometimes a product of our own making.

A wrestling coach who accepts a position in a middle school, high school or in some college situations often finds himself negotiating for practice space and is quite often limited in the time he is able to secure practice sessions in our educational facilities. These issues are prevalent in many situations across the country. Some coaches have the benefit and the luxury of having two gyms, which helps ease potential conflicts. And in rare cases, some even have a wrestling room or a facility that is designated for the purpose of the wrestling team exclusively. This is a very unusual occurrence.

As a former head wrestling coach in North Carolina, I am very familiar with the popularity and the emphasis placed on basketball by the administration, the student body, and the community. I love all sports. And, in many cases, basketball and football pay the bulk of the athletic bills. My experience as a high school athletic director, assistant varsity football coach, assistant principal, and high school principal have given me plenty of opportunity to mull over and debate the balance of funding. Issues related to this scenario can, in some cases, have a negative or inequitable impact on wrestling and other sports that might be presumed to have less profitable gate receipts.

The best remedy for this situation will be to work hard at ensuring the credibility, validity, and professional attributes of your program. It will be very difficult for any administrator to ignore what your program brings to the success, and to the image of your school, if you are doing things the way that they can and should be done. In fact, if you plan your program effectively there should be plenty of opportunity to not only foot your own bill, but to be able to speak from a position of power because of the money you will able to make above and beyond what it costs for uniforms and officials. This is not to suggest that you should always have to pay your own way. But you will find that it will be difficult for the people who control the purse strings to ignore your on-going work and contribution toward your own success.

If you work hard, plan well, and begin to improve the level of performance of your team, you will begin to be able to host legitimately strong tournaments, drawing greater crowds, better gates, and more publicity to your program. The increased parent participation that will grow out of your efforts will also have a positive impact on the negotiating potential that you will have with the school administration. When you have to go to the Athletic Director with a request to take an overnight trip to ensure a productive level of competition, you will want to be equipped with the advantages that you will have accumulated because of your exceptional efforts in making your own way.

The momentum that you will gain in terms of wins, publicity, and financial stability will begin to grow past the previous expectations and limitations of the wrestling programs at your school in the past eras. The administration and booster clubs are often taken aback by the eruption of financial results and requests for additional funds that accompany the growth of what you will begin to create in wrestling. It can be a very exciting and sometimes controversial time during the birth of your program. Your success will provide credibility and bargaining power.

Unfortunately, in some situations, I have seen coaches and wrestlers take a negative approach toward changing their perceived position as a "stepchild" with funding and facility issues. It is far better and more professional to take the high road toward improving the limitations and conflicts that can occur between various sports and among coaches. Some choose to descend toward criticizing other programs, sometimes inspiring, or at least tolerating friction between athletes, or bad-mouthing administrators for what they perceive as having been slighted on the funding when compared with the amounts enjoyed by other sports.

There is no doubt about the fact that your sport deserves as much, or more, as any other sport at your school. And if you are not going to take a strong stand to ensure the success of your program, then you can be sure that no one else will. But there will be little advantage for you, or your wrestlers, by taking the low road in an effort to gain greater benefits for your team.

There has always been a healthy competition and a fair amount of teasing between basketball players and wrestlers because of the close association between seasons and facilities. But that should be the extent of the disagreements. I have normally been able to have great friendships with basketball coaches because of the necessary level of communication that you should attempt to seek, in order to create an atmosphere of professionalism.

You should expect to be able to have frank discussions about what is in the best interest of both the wrestlers and the basketball players. In most circumstances, you will find that you will have much to gain by being a strong voice for your program, while promoting the opportunities of other sports secondary only to wrestling. I have always encouraged all of my wrestlers to support other athletes in the school at every opportunity.

In fact, there can also be great advantages in encouraging your athletes to participate in other sports when they are not wrestling. Some wrestlers make tremendous gains by participating in club wrestling and off-season tournaments. But there is also a great deal to be gained by encouraging them to participate in other sports at the school, if they are not going to be on the mat at those times in the off-season. Any time a teenager can be spending two hours a day in an organized, competitive activity that includes supervision by a professional adult, they are not on the street getting in trouble, and not on the couch drinking soft drinks and eating honey buns.

Another complication is the comparison between amateur and professional wrestling. At least now, in recent years, there has been a little more distinguishable line drawn between the two activities than there was, only a few years ago, when professional wrestling actually professed to be a competitive sport.

Most professional wrestling stars though great athletes in their own right, perform a scripted scenario of dramatic and entertaining skits. They execute acrobatic displays of volatility and action that have less to do with finding out if the best man wins, and more to do with immersing an electrified audience of loyal fans in a heated arena of a larger than life animated conflicts. Granted there are probably quite a few of us that have been closet professional wrestling fans at one time or another, and most of us have spent a little time in front of the TV set viewing a bit of this prescribed excitement and drama.

Professional Wrestling is a successful business that is used to promote the extravagant lifestyles and livelihoods of a few and a powerful entertainment resource for many. But for the average Joe on the street, professional wrestling sometimes either exaggerates viewer expectations of amateur wrestling or it inhibits the participation on the part of some potential amateur wrestling fans. And, it may distract from their investment in the initial time it takes to see, to learn, and to appreciate the real drama, risk taking, and personal levels of courage, that are performed at the amateur levels of wrestling competition.

This minor interference that can be created by the professionals can sometimes affect the efforts of amateur wrestlers to be taken seriously. Our attempts to take the high road can sometimes be derailed or minimized by influences outside of our own doing.

I would be less than accurate with my descriptions of professional wrestling if I did not acknowledge a new effort to give legitimacy to what is known as "real professional wrestling." There has been an effort on the part of amateur wrestling at the upper levels of the sport to create another professional league that really does incorporate an honest and sincere level of competition among hopeful Olympians, and post-college athletes, as a way of helping them fund their efforts to train for future competitions, while promoting the amateur ranks.

Part of the motivation for the new professional league appears to have been created as a way to help support world-class athletes as they prepare to represent our country in the World Games, and in the next Summer Olympic Games. Some of these matches have been broadcast on the Cable Sports Networks and could be a beneficial promotion toward spreading a level of understanding and popularity about amateur wrestling.

The greatest opportunities to ensure a strong public posture of the importance and the legitimacy of amateur wrestlers comes with the daily expressions of confidence, professionalism, and successful performance on the mat, in the classroom, and in the community. The way coaches and teams carry themselves on a daily basis, how they operate in the school environment, and how they compose themselves as they represent their school, will impact how you and they are treated with regard to praise and respect.

Carlos Hough, Point Andrews High School, 3x Finalist 1x State Champ-Coached by Wally Burke.

Taking the high road will not always be the easiest way to deal with the difficulties and inequities that will surely arise as you make your way toward the credibility and distinction that you and your wrestlers will deserve and desire. But, working hard to stay above any kind of defensive or negative fray will be the best way to establish the kind of legacy that will sustain long-term success, and equip your program with the attributes that will build the foundation you will need to create a dynasty in this sport.

22

Identities

*B*ob Hilfiger was a wrestler at Appalachian State when I *got there. He was from New York. He had a raspy and abrasive voice that projected like a cannon. The truth is he scared me a little bit, not because he was a big guy, I think he wrestled about 142. But he was a little like a time bomb. You could not really predict when he might erupt into a burst of aggressive commentary or explode into physical animation. He could be crude and he was a vicious competitor on the mat. He had a take no prisoners' attitude that served him well. He was as extreme as anyone I had ever met at that time in my life.*

One night after practice I had been overdoing it with my workouts on the mat and in the weight room and ended up passing out in the locker room. When I began to get my bearings back, Bob helped me into his jeep and we plowed through the snow in Boone to get me to the infirmary. I found out that I had an over-secretion of lactic acid in my blood that was soon corrected. But we spent some time talking that night as we figured out what was going on and Bob turned out to be as caring and concerned as anyone I had met. I learned to appreciate his intensive approach to life.

Rob Heaton was a two time state champion at the 189lb weight class at West Henderson High School in both 1992 and 1993. He was not like anyone else I had ever coached. He was a physical beast. He had made it to the semi-finals of the state tournament as a sophomore in the year before he won it the first time. He was very talented and a brilliant student. He carried near a 4.0 academically and in the off season had hair down to his shoulders. And we agreed that he would not wear the earring on campus at least during the months of wrestling season. Some of you are thinking, "how conservative is that?" But, I did demand a certain level of discipline and uniformity as a part of the requirement for my team back in those days.

Rob also continuously wore a skull and cross bones necklace around his massive neck when he wasn't on the mat. And the music he listened to was primarily hard and loud heavy metal. The two groups that stand out in my mind were Motley Crue and Metallica. The truth is that after spending so much time with him and watching him operate in his efforts to be successful on the mat, some of his music even began to grow on me. He cared deeply about our team and the individuals that were on it. He forced me to have an open mind about some of his extreme characteristics due in part because of the lengths he went to learn what I was trying to teach.

Group of West Henderson High wrestlers celebrating after a tournament victory in 1989.

The dynamics in wrestling, whether it is in the conduct of individual matches, or in the in the way the sport is designed for competition in scholastic, collegiate, and even Olympic tournaments has always attracted the rugged individualist. And, it also creates strong opportunities for athletes to experience the benefits of having been an important part of a team concept. These attributes have clear benefits for preparing individuals to make important contributions to their vocations, families and social organizations.

But there may be an element of interest related to this game of wrestling that is not often well defined or capitalized on at least in a formal way. Having been a middle school, high school, and a collegiate wrestler, as well as a successful wrestling coach and a school administrator, has given me many opportunities to observe the social and cultural behaviors that give rise to the public perception of this sport.

Whether it is deserved or not, wrestling tends to be associated with an image that suggests that we often inherit and develop some very unique and diverse personalities as we migrate through the ranks of what this sport has to offer. Even at the college level, some wrestlers acquire personal habits and behaviors that are sometimes misunderstood by the average population of students. Many wrestlers do tend to take on some pretty extreme traits of work ethic, emotional concentration, and a pervasive element of risk taking as they work toward their goals. This phenomenon sometimes creates a mystique about the game that unfortunately establishes boundaries that can lead to questions about whether some individuals would be willing to pursue a chance to participate in the sport. But in reality, most of these eccentric behaviors, obsessive or compulsive rituals and idiosyncrasies are probably found among athletes in other sports.

The individual nature of wrestling provides considerable opportunities for the visible expression of these behaviors. The fact that there are no helmets or pads, and the view of the wrestling mat is so up-close and personal, increases and highlights the chance for fans and other athletes to make presumptions and assessments about the extreme characteristics and personalities of the competitors on the mat that are far less observable and dramatic in other sports.

Other considerations and deliberations about the wrestling game that sometimes affect the clientele of potential candidates can include a simple refusal by some young men to wear a singlet, because they think it is too skimpy or revealing. I understand that swim teams have had some of the same recruiting problems. But I guess some people that are truly insecure about the appearance of their physique might actually have a problem with this concern.

Other issues that can single out wrestlers include our apparent lack of discretion about putting our hands on other men. Clearly, in this sport, if you expect to survive, you will be required to end up in some pretty intimate looking positions, even as violent, and as masculine as the action will actually have to be during the matches. So there are some significant issues and misinterpretations about the game that lead some people to their own confusing assessments about wrestlers in general.

I have coached many students who would have never seriously considered completing their high school diplomas had it not been for their vested interest and their excited level of participation in the wrestling program. Their passion for what was offered in wrestling outweighed their lack of interest in school, and helped to break an on-going family tradition of dropping out of school. Their success in wrestling changed not only their lives, but the lives of their children. In other cases, mine included, wrestling offered an attitude and an avenue for many athletes to become motivated to apply and participate at the university level that would not have been considered had they not gained a sense of confidence and success in a wrestling program.

When you consider the mentality of some people, it should be obvious why this sport can become attractive to meeting the needs of one particular troublesome way of thinking that is often experienced by large numbers of adolescents and teenagers in this country. You don't have to look far to see how starved many young people are for attention. There behaviors often define an obvious and an irresistible need to be accepted and associated with a group of people who will value their contribution to an organization, or a chance to fulfill an opportunity to be accepted.

These young people feverishly seek ways to be celebrated and glorified by the other members of the gang, or organization, whether it is for good deeds, or for incidences of negative risk-taking that will ensure their status with somebody who cares. The rags, colors, and styles of fashion that are used to highlight and identify gang membership or social acceptance could be replaced with an athletic uniform, and a wrestling headgear. This kind of transformation can only take place in an environment where a coach or a significant adult takes the time to find creative ways to articulate the right promotion and recruiting process in a wrestling program.

There are windows of opportunity that are sometimes missed in student's lives, when they are truly impressionable and vulnerable. At these times, it can be the lure of either good, or sometimes bad, invitations that accompany their hunger to be recognized with something, or someone, larger than their own personal identity. This need can often be a met with a positive experience like the rewards and fellowship that are offered and associated with a self-esteem building program, like a wrestling team. Or, on the other hand, this dire need to be accepted can become littered with negative, or unproductive associations, and experiences that quickly welcome these young people into the ranks of mediocre ambition, street status, or even the drug culture.

There are many examples of young men who have either turned away from a negative situation to participate in wrestling, or have avoided engaging in delinquent activities altogether because of their participation in this demanding game. Their newfound passion for the sport and their efforts to maintain their status as an individual competitor, or as a team-member in wrestling, can often provide the leverage needed to guide them past the bad situations. Most coaches can cite examples of times when they have had these types of kids in their programs.

J.J. Davis was a student at Byrnes High School in South Carolina. He is a 2x SC State Champion, and he is a member of the Strong and Courageous Club. He was recently recruited to participate as a member of the Wrestling Team at the University of North Carolina, at Pembroke by Coach P.J. Smith. He is an exceptional athlete and a quality individual. J.J.'s high school coach was Eric Hansen.

This whole preceding commentary may sound a little romantic or idealistic. But, there are many adult-run educational institutions and athletic organizations that have failed to recognize the value of tapping into this need, or this thirst, for being identified as special, or at least recognized as an important element of an organized or unified group. Some coaches probably haven't spent a lot of time sorting out the parallels associated with what young people want and what we have to offer. But, this sport gives students a choice, and a resource, when orchestrated with precision, that will have a powerful and demonstrative affect on who they are, and what they will eventually contribute to society.

Wrestling coaches have the potential to create what these young people need. That is why it is so important for you to promote your program in a way that highlights the advantages of what is really available to the participants that commit to your program.

Often times, there are some brilliant kids in the middle schools, and high schools, that have personal obstacles, either real, or imagined, that will melt away, if you can find a way to get them into a genuinely successful wrestling program. Some are affected by their situations in poverty, limited by a lack of transportation, and inhibited by parents who do not see the value in wrestling, or any other athletic or extra-curricular activities.

This sport creates an arena that allows some of these young people to see a clear avenue of potential success and self-promotion, that they can clearly visualize and pursue without the outside interruptions, and the political frameworks, or biased interferences, that most have learned to contend with in their normal lives.

Cameron McDowell as a sophomore at East Henderson High School. He is coached by Barry Cannon and assistant coach Travis Hannah at East Henderson High School, and he is a member of the Strong and Courageous Wrestling Club, Coached by Norman Osteen. The photo is from a tournament at Byrnes High School in S.C. in December of 2005.

Whether the students are rich or poor wrestling can create a dynamic that serves everyone's need to have a hand in forging their own personal destiny. And, it allows them to make a contribution toward a greater good or team goal, while pursuing what can become an avenue of personal triumph.

Rob Heaton celebrates his victory with Coach McDowell in Greensboro, North Carolina after winning his second NCHSAA State Championship Title at the 189lb weight class in 1993.

When the bags are packed and each competitor crawls on a bus to head toward a chance to engage in an actual wrestling match, all social, economic, and political differences are cast aside. Each young athlete will look, act, and pretty much feel the same way about who they are, after going through your program. Their mission defines their status, and their uniforms identify their brand of intensive potential. If you have done your job as a competent and caring coach, your wrestlers will embrace the ride to the arena and welcome the process of drumming up the courage needed to face their opponents. They will be excited with anticipation about the contest, well equipped to face the physical, mental, and emotional challenge that lies ahead.

23

Communication, Opportunities and Resources

In recent years, because of changes in technology, many tools have evolved that can be used as exceptional motivational, strategic, and visionary accessories for ensuring your team's ultimate success as a competitive program throughout the year, and in your final potential to compete at the State Tournament.

During the last thirty years that I've been wrestling, coaching, or working with young people in the sport, these changes have been phenomenal. One of the greatest advantages to coaches and wrestlers has been the increased accessibility to opportunities for communication. As a high school wrestler in the late 1970's there were few chances to gain information, statistics or general commentary about wrestlers and teams outside of your own county or region. And, it was impossible to find out much about competitive results and statistics with regard to a potential opponent in other parts of the state or country.

In the old days, coaches were left to inspire work ethics, clarify levels of state championship caliber performances in other areas, and generate a high level of enthusiasm about improving skill levels without the benefit of the publicity, propaganda, and motivation lists that exist today.

Athletes and coaches can now not only gain a wide variety of pertinent information about the merits and accomplishments of future opponents, but they can have a constant opportunity to be immersed in the spirit and commentary on the sport, to a degree that could not have been imagined even a short time ago. Details and statistical data that are available on a variety of websites on the Internet and results from competitions from all over the country are highlighted in written publications and newspapers at an arm's length. Even TV, radio, and hometown newspapers do a little better job of carrying information and covering special events that are related to wrestling in today's technologically advanced world.

One outstanding element of wrestling coverage that helps immerse athletes and coaches in the news and literature of amateur wrestling is the individual and team rankings that are established by various media organizations. The first list of rankings that were viewed with a great deal of legitimacy in North Carolina began to gain momentum in the 1970's when Bob Mauldin, at that time a school administrator, created a written publication called the "Mat News" that became and exceptional instrument for enlightening young wrestling hopefuls.

As a young coach, I became aware of the "Mat News" in the Mid-1980's. I will never forget finding my first top-twenty team ranking that was highlighted on the front page of this well-circulated publication. At that time I was a twenty-two year-old head coach at a school then called Madison-

Mayodan High School (now called McMichael) in Rockingham County, North Carolina. At that time there was no division of categories with regard to the alignment of school classifications. All North Carolina teams were considered in the construction of the one single motivation list. What that "Mat News" motivation list did for me as a coach, and for my athletes as wrestlers, clearly motivated my sense of responsibility and ambition to continue raising the level of status in my program. The widespread coverage inspired my efforts to continue the successful publicity for my team and for our school.

This measured comparison and the published list of superlatives heavily affected the ambition and improved the performance of our athletes. The added attention to our program helped to substantiate the benefits of the hard work we were doing and created a rich sense of hope and ambition about further establishing the stature of our team. The notoriety displayed in the "Mat News" was very beneficial to our progress as a team. As we began to climb further up the listed rankings, it inspired our work and enhanced our posture in the community, in the state, and in the amateur wrestling world.

Bob Mauldin, Editor of the "NC Mat News" Amateur Wrestling Publication. Photo was taken while he was receiving an award presented at the NCAA Championships in St. Louis, MO for "Publication of the Year" awarded by the National Wrestling Media Association, and he also recently received the "Lifetime Service Award" in the "National Wrestling Hall of Fame" in Stillwater, Oklahoma.

The sense of legitimacy that came with being ranked in the state, and the commentary that was distributed about our team, and others, helped to arm our athletes with a sound level of motivation and knowledge, while encouraging a perceived sense of prowess, and a status that helped our individual wrestlers to identify the importance of their position on the team, and their position of perceived credibility in the state.

Coaches who embrace the potential coverage of an athlete's opportunities to be recognized will equip themselves with the developmental tools needed for improving skill levels and inspiring the competitive growth of their team. Attention to this instructional tool will often create a heightened sense of commitment, and a focused ambition by your wrestlers to seek superlative levels of success in the wrestling game.

On a national level, before the benefit of the on-line opportunities that now exist for gaining information about wrestling, most athletes and coaches once turned to the "Amateur Wrestling News" and the "Wrestling USA Magazine" to gain tidbits of information about Olympic, collegiate, and high school articles of commentary related to the sport. Both publications are still important and competitive forms of media coverage in the world of amateur wrestling. These magazines are now available on the internet and have helped to establish a broad-based opportunity for moving the sport forward all over America. They were both at one time an absolute necessity for finding the scarce information that was out there in the early days.

As a wrestler myself during the late 1970's and early 1980's, we were all starved for whatever we could get our hands on to help immerse our minds and connect our passions with others who had this same love of competition, and the understood level of pride in the benefits of this great sport.

Today's athletes, my son included, spend a great deal of time on the Internet looking at rankings, finding off-season Freestyle and Greco-Roman tournaments, and reading about the feats and records of those individuals and teams in the sport that are carrying on the strong traditions and new challenges. These results are far more available to my son than they ever were for me as a high school, or college wrestler, or even in my early days as a coach.

Organizations and publications like the "Mat News", ncmat.com, and numerous websites for club teams, along with a variety of publications from amateur wrestling federations and organizations that promote up-coming Free-Style and Greco Roman tournaments, have become a staple to the game. All of these resources have become important supplements for coaches and competitors in the amateur wrestling world today.

David Barker

David Barker has begun to establish himself as one of the outstanding go-to people with regard to wrestling communications that are currently available to the masses of interested readers seeking some of the most recent and legitimate information associated with the sport of wrestling. His motivation list has been a powerful tool for generating enthusiasm across the state and the nation. The list, called "The Super 32," and can be found at the ncmat.com website.

Cameron McDowell, checking out the www.ncmat.com site on the computer.

The list is generated as a powerful tool for ranking the competitors and serves as a promotion for what has become an outstanding preseason tournament called the Super 32 Challenge. Participation in the event has grown by leaps and bounds during each of the years since its inception. The tournament has been held five of the last six years at Morehead High School in Eden North Carolina.

David has consistently and enthusiastically promoted the tournament and utilized the benefit of the "NC Mat" Website to encourage the participation of wrestlers all over the state and across the country by creating, advertising and attending to the motivation list that highlights the potential standouts in the amateur ranks. David is a resident of Eden, North Carolina. He has a strong background in the sport. His father, Wayne Barker, is a fine man and was an outstanding high school coach in North Carolina in his own right.

The Super 32 has become so popular that it has outgrown even the very large high school facilities at Morehead Eden High School. The new location of the tournament, at the larger venue, was first used in the fall of 2005. This event is already beginning to be recognized as one of the fastest growing amateur wrestling contests in the nation, giving students from North Carolina, and all over the country, the opportunity to refine their skills in a competitive environment of intensive wrestling as they begin to prescribe their early vision for success and their preseason hopes.

Many wrestlers anxiously await the measured publicity and the recognition of the possible opponents that are highlighted with Mr. Barker's effective contribution to the improved levels of communication found in amateur wrestling. David's hard work and attention to detail, combined with the benefit of the publicity organized by Sarah Koenig at the NC Mat website, the Super 32 has become so popular that the tournament has been moved to the much larger site at the Greensboro Coliseum Complex in Greensboro, North Carolina.

Frank Rader

In the state of North Carolina and across the nation, the USA Wrestling Organization frequently informs potential grapplers about upcoming amateur wrestling events. The organization regularly clarifies details associated with registrations, weigh-ins and changes in the various sites from year to year, as their annual tournaments are scheduled throughout the country.

Frank Rader has been a long time participant and an organizer in the USA Wrestling Association. He has served in almost every capacity of the organization at one time or another. He is credited with providing a level of stability in the financial structure of the association over the years, and he is currently serving as Board Treasurer in North Carolina. At one point in his long history with USA Wrestling he served as a National Level Administrator, acting as the "Executive Director" for the National Organization for a short time.

Frank Rader, NC USA Wrestling Association Administrator. He has been inducted as a member of the "National Wrestling Hall of Fame" for his extensive contributions to the sport. He is a recipient of a "Lifetime Service Award."

Frank has long provided a level of stability and a consistent source of opportunity for young people to wrestle and compete beyond their scholastic competitions. He often shows up in different parts of the state to administrate tournaments by piloting his own aircraft. He has served in a very strategic and effective capacity as a member of the USA Wrestling Organization for many years.

Frank's contribution, along with the effective work of Phil Sherrill, who is serving as the current State Chairman in North Carolina, has been supported by many volunteers and participating members that have worked together to enhance the growth of a variety of wrestling opportunities in the state. The NC USA Wrestling Tournaments have helped to ensure the success of many motivated competitors who are searching for ways to improve their craft in the sport.

NHSCA

Another opportunity to gain experience for amateur wrestlers is provided by the National High School Coaching Association. The administrative body of the NHSCA sponsors events in the nation that tend to have exceptional draws of participation. Their very successful tournament that is held at Virginia Beach every June, provides an accessible opportunity for Carolina kids to gain experience in a National Competition.

There are increasing numbers of wrestling tournaments and improved accessibility to professionally run instructional programs such as the Ken Chertow camps. These organizations are providing consistent promotions and advertising techniques that create local and national networks of enthusiasm and wrestling opportunities that were not always available. These activities are beginning to establish communities of passionate participation from individuals that are looking for skillful instruction and a chance to compete beyond their scholastic competitions. Increased participation in these activities and others will help ensure future interest and success in the sport.

24

Collegiate Resources for Coaches and Kids

The first three weeks I spent in the wrestling room at Pembroke State University was the most eye opening experience of my life. It was here that I found out how little I really knew about wrestling. The depth of this experience forced me to take a hard at look myself and required me to make some adult decisions about what I had really gotten myself into with wrestling at the college level. It was more demanding physically, intellectually and emotionally than anything I had ever done.

I supposed at the time that with Mike Olson as the head coach at this institution and with all the suffering that was taking place, the regiment had to be something comparable to boot camp. The other complicating factor was the fact that I had gone through high school without establishing any kind of standardized approach to studying. I spent the first month in college going to class, going to practice, going to eat, to study and to bed. But, I did actually begin to get a grasp on the academics. In fact, I think the discipline of wrestling actually helped me with establishing a strict plan for developing the study habits I needed to find success in the classroom.

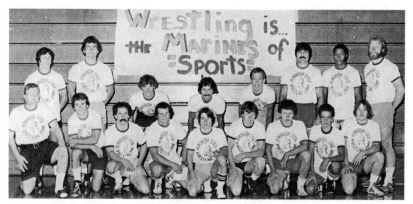

1979 Pembroke State University Wrestling Camp: Coaches and College Counselors. Back row, left to right: Matt Lynch, B.D. LaPrade, Steve LaPrade, Bill Stevens, Marty Tolleson, Billy Starks, Evert Neal and Greg Frey. Front Row: Head Coach at PSU-Mike Olson, 2nd to right unnamed counselor, Mike Stanbridge, unnamed national champion clinician, Joe Robinson, Billy Warren, Darrell McDowell, Jeff Torres and another unnamed counselor on the end.

The flat and hot environment in the coastal plains was also an adjustment for a country boy like me. As I began to acquaint myself with the culture at Pembroke State I found myself to be a little bit of an oddity. In the beginning, except for at wrestling practice, I was a little uncomfortable and homesick. But I loved the wrestling. I slowly began to make progress on the mat to the point of competing successfully with the other team members around my weight class. But there was always stiff competition from beasts like Barry and Gary Dean, a couple of massive physical specimens, and Greg Shealy, a 190lb. NAIA All American from Irmo High School in South Carolina who tended to keep me humble as I attempted to establish myself in the practice room. I was amazed and excited by the repertoire of moves and strategies that were made available from the coaching staff to the members of the PSU team. The skull sessions and the distribution of printed materials for improving skills were an effective part of the program. The collection of handbooks would later be a beneficial part of what I would use to organize my own high school practices as a coach.

At one point when I was concerned about getting back to the mountains, during that first semester, I contacted Paul Mance, who was the Head Coach at Appalachian State about transferring to ASU in Boone, NC. Like the day I showed up for college at PSU on a Trailways bus, I had never been there or even seen the university before. But, I knew that it was in the mountains, that they had wrestling, and that it couldn't be as hot as it was in September in Pembroke. All I had was a pay phone on the outside of a brick wall on the Jacobs Hall dormitory. That was where I did all of my business and organized all my communications with Appalachian State or anywhere else in the world I attempted to contact. I finally heard back from Coach Mance at ASU who initially stated that I might get to come to Boone in January of my freshmen year. I was thrilled. I later received a communication from his office stating that unfortunately it would be August of my sophomore year before I could attend. I remember going back to my room that afternoon and squalling like a big old baby. About a week later Mance contacted me himself and said that my financial aid had come through and I was back on my way to the mountains in January if I still wanted to come.

I still had most of the semester to experience life on the Pembroke State campus. I met many friendly students and started going to the dances at the student union on campus almost every Saturday night, and sometimes I would even venture up into town for a sandwich. I usually took a friend *and we went up to a place that was a combination pool hall and sub shop. Many of the people from Pembroke had a Lumbee Indian Heritage. And they often spoke with a dialect that was much different from what you might hear anywhere else in the country. When I got there I would often hear tales about social friction and political conflicts related to past failures on the part of the Lumbee people to be recognized and legitimately considered as a tribe of Native Americans. I had even heard that some of locals claimed to be descendents of "The Lost Colony." I have to admit the racial issues made me a little nervous.*

I finally had the bright idea that I wanted to go to church one Sunday in the town of Pembroke. I convinced a friend of mine from New York that was on the wrestling team, named Alan Jameson to go with me. He asked if I had ever been there before and I said, "It's a church. How bad could it be?" So we got dressed that morning and we met in the courtyard in front of Jacobs Hall. By the time we walked down the street to the little brick building with big white doors we were already late for the service. Neither of us were Methodists, but the chapel was within walking distance, so we had agreed that it would serve the purpose. We walked up the concrete steps and entered the double doors almost simultaneously. Everyone else was already seated. A man in the back got up and ushered us to two of the last seats that were left in the house.

As we settled into the sermon Alan leaned over and in his in deep voice and New York accent, asked me, "Have you noticed that you are the only white man in this building and I'm the only black man?" And then he grinned. I honestly had not noticed until he mentioned it. As we left the church and talked to the people on the way out of the building, everyone in the congregation of what appeared to be Lumbee Indians could not have been nicer than they were that day. After being nervous about going uptown on Saturday nights, it was great to find out that these people were just like the rest of us on Sunday.

By the time I finished the semester at PSU, I almost began to question my decision about transferring to Boone. I had really improved my skills in wrestling. I had also discovered that there was room for a social life in college. I had begun to develop some rich friendships with several of the students at Pembroke like Freddie Richards and Chuck Jones, two high school state champions from the low country of South Carolina, who spoke with a heavy "Geechee" accent. None of us had a car but the two of them had a black and white TV in their room. I remember watching an Earnest Borgnine horror movie in their room late one Saturday night on a weekend when hardly anyone else was left on campus. We were all scared to death, but it was a good time.

I also met Cecil Mock while I was there. He was a charismatic member of the wrestling team who is now a well-respected wrestling official in North Carolina. He is also a coach and a successful middle school language arts teacher. Cecil referees the action at the NCHSAA State Tournament each year.

Most Saturday nights a dance would be sponsored in the small student union by a student group or club. It was 1979 and there was plenty of disco music to go around. And rap music was just beginning to take hold. So I was getting an education in lots of things as I found my way around the dance floor and what was available on the social scene on the Pembroke campus at that time.

A dramatic experience that happened during that time was the Iran hostage crisis. I'll never forget the feeling I had when students from all over the campus were gathered in the student union to watch the news as it came in with the details of what was going on in the middle east on the TV screen. It had the same kind of feel to it as 9/11, especially when I was so far away from home. There were students that were really cranked up about the ordeal. Some of them were expressing their fears and their anger in a very emotional and public display on the campus. Many were discussing the images on the screen and some were even talking about quitting school and signing up for the military. We were very close to the Fort Bragg area and that seemed to encourage an even more dramatic atmosphere of concern about the crisis. It was the first time that I had ever really thought deeply about that kind of international conflict as an eighteen year old.

I learned as much wrestling as I could absorb that fall. I made friends that I would have for the rest of my life. I found out that the winters in Pembroke, North Carolina are very nice, and I even found out how to get to "South of the Border."

At the end of that fall semester during my freshmen year I did leave Pembroke State University, but it was from an experience that I would eventually come to view as one of the most important and significant times of my entire life. The impact on my level of maturity and the views I formed have been invaluable in my career and have truly enriched my personal life.

When January finally came, I packed up my army trunk and headed for the high country and to Appalachian State University to start the whole process over again. On the day the semester started in the spring of 1980, I hitched a ride with a friend from Hendersonville and went to the financial aid office at ASU where I met Steve Gabriel, former head wrestling coach at Appalachian State, who became my advisor. He sent me to a dorm room on the 2nd floor of Justice Hall and I was off to a whole new adventure. As I passed Grandfather Mountain that day for the first time and saw the snow on its rocky peaks, I had little doubt or any question about the impulsive action I had taken to get me where I thought I wanted to be.

Paul Mance

Paul Mance has 28 years of experience and over 300 wins as the head coach at Appalachian State University in Boone, North Carolina, at his college Alma Mater. During his tenure, the Mountaineers have remained at, or near, the top of the league rankings in Southern Conference Competition. He has great pride in the program at ASU and he has worked very hard for many years to ensure the stability of what has become an on-going tradition of success.

Coach Paul Mance, Head Coach at Appalachian State University.

The summer wrestling camp at Appalachian State University is one of the largest camps in the nation, and yet it provides effective individual instruction to each camp member. Wrestlers drill and compete at their appropriate skill levels before participating in a very competitive tournament event near the end of each week.

The visiting coaches are invited to participate in furthering their level of knowledge and understanding about what is new and effective for ensuring the success of their high school and middle school teams. The consistent and historical attention to serving the coaches in the area by Coach Mance and the ASU wrestling program has paid tremendous dividends to quality of amateur wrestling in North Carolina and all over the Southeast.

Photo of Appalachian State University and the town of Boone, North Carolina from Howard's Knob Mountain.

Steve Gabriel

There were several outstanding coaches preceding the success that has been enjoyed by Paul Mance and his staff of assistant coaches. One exceptional head coach that led the ASU program very effectively and helped to substantiate a strong foundation of wrestling success for the Mountaineers was Steve Gabriel.

In the years before Coach Gabriel started his successful era as the head coach at ASU, he was also the head coach at Appalachian High School in Boone, NC, where from 1957 through 1965 he won 8 out of 9 NCHSAA State Championships, and he had numerous undefeated seasons. Gabriel later worked as an administrator at the university in the financial aid department for several years after retiring his post as head coach. It was an honor for me to have been able to work with Steve Gabriel as my financial aid advisor during the early 1980's, when I was a student at ASU. I had the privilege of speaking with him on many occasions and talking to him about wrestling. He was still very enthusiastic about the experiences he had enjoyed during his days as a wrestling coach.

The coaches that preceded Gabriel at ASU included "Red" Watkins, who had been a legend as the head coach at ASU for decades. He led the Mountaineer wrestling program very successfully for many years in the early days of the wrestling program at Appalachian State. Watkins was a well-known figure in the amateur wrestling world throughout the nation for his contribution to the sport.

There were a number of coaches that held the program together following Watkins' retirement. Joe Edminston ran the team during the 1959-60 wrestling season. And, Buddy Chandler filled in for one year during the 1960-61 season. Frank "Dutch" Meyer took over the program the next year and began establishing another line of successful victories just prior to Gabriel's arrival on the scene as the head coach for the Mountaineers during the mid-1960's. Each of these men made significant contributions to what has become a rich historical past in the sport of wrestling at Appalachian State University.

After Coach Gabriel's retirement from the game in the early 1970's, he was replaced by Ken Koenig for a two year period. Paul Mance then secured the head coaching position after Koenig, and he has been in charge of the successful program ever since.

Coach Gabriel was recently inducted and recognized as a member of the North Carolina chapter of the National Wrestling Hall of Fame, in Stillwater, Oklahoma with a Lifetime Service Award in the Sport of Wrestling.

The cumulative effect of the efforts that have been made by Appalachian State to recruit athletes and work with coaches from the southern region has made a significant impact on the coaches in the Carolinas and in the surrounding area. The groundswell of interest in coaching wrestling that has emerged from ASU can probably be attributed to the fact the university was once a teacher's college. The other element in the formula clearly includes the rich learning experiences from time spent on the mat, and the success that most of the athletes have found in the Mountaineer program.

As young men are educated and motivated in an environment that provides high quality wrestling techniques, and they become immersed as members in this type of fraternal experience, they often choose to become coaches. After they graduate from college, many Appalachian State University wrestlers are redistributed into the various high schools across the state where they begin to establish pockets of pride and success in their sport among the members of their given communities.

Appalachian State has always had a strong wrestling tradition. It has offered students from all over the nation the chance to gain an outstanding academic experience in the "high country" of the North Carolina, while participating in a competitive wrestling program. The university has become a "hot bed" for producing scores of coaches in the sport. The coaches that have emerged from the Mountaineer program have provided a high level of success and stability for amateur wrestling in the Carolinas and in surrounding states. Many of these coaching leaders have taken on "larger than life" status among their peers and within their communities with their efforts to contribute back to the sport of wrestling.

Appalachian State Summer Wrestling Camp 2005.

The dynamic that has been created because of the loyal return of these coaches to the wrestling culture at Appalachian State University, with their participation in the annual summer wrestling camps that are made available in Boone, and at some of the other universities across the state, has improved the overall quality of amateur wrestling in North Carolina and beyond.

Grandfather Mountain from Foscoe, North Carolina, near Boone.

There is a prevalent thread of contribution that can be found in the history of ASU wrestling that is sometimes overlooked in the scope of the process of what has occurred over the years in this sport. It is pretty amazing to see the entanglement of the lives and teams that have in some way been affected by what has grown out of amateur wrestling in Boone, North Carolina.

Jim Whitmer, left to right, fourth over on the bottom, and Paul Mance-left to right fourth over on the top in an ASU Team Photograph from 1967.

ASU, along with the University of North Carolina at Pembroke, have provided opportunities for ensuring the success of a mix of recruits from all over the nation, while providing the backbone of the collegiate efforts that have been made at giving attention to leaving the door open to the Carolina kids, who truly want to become successful at the university level of competition. ASU once participated in the NAIA League with much success and since that time they have been participating in Division I competition. The Mountaineers have sent a very respectable number of wrestlers to the NCAA Championships on a consistent basis.

Ike Anderson, Olympic Games Place Winner, Greco-Roman Wrestling in Seoul Korea 1988 and former Appalachian State Southern Conference Champ.

Ike Anderson has become one of Appalachian State University's most celebrated and successful athletes. He hails from Lower Richland High School in Columbia, South Carolina. Ike won a Southern Conference Title as a collegiate wrestler during his career in Boone before becoming an Assistant Coach at ASU. He was a very competitive wrestler, and he had a demanding style when he coached for the Mountaineers in the early 1980's.

Ike later qualified for the Greco Roman Division of the United States Olympic Team, posting a fourth place finish at the qualifier after overcoming a number of complicating physical injuries to secure a spot on the squad. He competed in the games in Seoul, Korea in 1988, at a time in his life when he was nearing the age of thirty. During his performance in Seoul, Ike defeated opponents from Poland, China and Morocco before ultimately facing the Gold medal winner from the Soviet Union.

Ike eventually finished a very respectable sixth place in the Olympic Games. He is an outstanding coach and technician and he is currently acting as the Developmental Coach for the USA Greco Roman Wrestling Team in Colorado Springs,

Colorado. He has set an excellent example and made a tremendous contribution to amateur wrestling in the South and across the nation. His expertise has provided a wealth of knowledge for volumes of athletes throughout the country.

P.J. Smith

Another great contribution to the game has been the consistent level of performance and success by the University of North Carolina at Pembroke. The Braves were known for having had exceptional success at the NAIA Division of competition for many years, winning numerous conference championships, and now they continue to enjoy tremendous success in the NCAA Division II Championships. Pembroke has several athletes that are currently ranked at the highest levels of their Division in the nation. And their team is ranked in the top ten universities in the nation for schools of their size and enrollment. Coach P.J. Smith is the very successful head coach at the University of North Carolina at Pembroke.

Curry Pickard is in the dark head gear in the top position. He wrestled for Greg Frey at Morehead Eden where he accumulated a high school record of 207-15. Curry was a NCHSAA State Champion at the 119 pound weight class in the year 2000 and he was the MVP of the NCHSAA State Tournament as a champion again at 125lbs. in 2001. He was a USA Wrestling All American in 2001 and he has been an All American at the University of North Carolina at Pembroke during the 2003, 2004 and 2005 seasons. He was an NCAA Division II National Runner-up during the 2005 season. Curry Pickard's coach at UNCP is P.J. Smith.

P.J. Smith, Head Coach at the University of North Carolina at Pembroke.

Gardner Webb University under the direction of Head Coach Dick Wince, along with Campbell College, the University of North Carolina at Greensboro, the Citadel, Davidson, Duke, and a handful of other small colleges in North and South Carolina, such as Winston Salem State, Anderson College have also been able to provide opportunities and avenues of wrestling success for a number of students in the southeastern part of the nation that might have otherwise been overlooked.

Bill Lam

A limited number of Carolina kids, but often those wrestlers that have enjoyed the most exceptional success at the high school level in our state, have competed effectively in the Atlantic Coast Conference. Many of these athletes have been recruited at the University of North Carolina at Chapel Hill in a program that has long been successful under the direction of former Head Coach Bill Lam. Lam is another exceptional wrestling coach who was recently inducted with a Lifetime Service Award in the National Hall of Fame for Wrestling. The Tar Heel program has just recently been taken over by former Carolina Tar Heel standout, and NCAA National Champion, C.D. Mock.

Bob Guzzo

Other exceptional high school wrestlers in the state have found a similar rate of success in the ACC under the long-time direction of Bob Guzzo, at North Carolina State University in Raleigh. Coach Guzzo retired just last year. Former Wolf Pack wrestler, Carter Jordan, who served in an interim capacity during this past year, and was recently confirmed as the permanent replacement in Raleigh, will replace him. It will be interesting to follow the recruiting practices for both of these new head coaches as they begin to impact the North Carolina wrestling culture as they coordinate their esteemed new jobs with the Tar Heels and the Wolf Pack in the Atlantic Coast Conference Wrestling League.

Even fewer North and South Carolina athletes have been recruited at the Division I Universities in other areas of the nation. But, as the level of skill has continued to improve across the state, and in the southeast, especially in recent years, a growing number of Carolina kids are beginning to find their way to improved levels of success in the ranks of amateur wrestling and coaching. There are now a few of the small-school division universities in this part of the country who have just recently decided to add wrestling programs to their lists of extra-curricular college activities. This should help create new opportunities for both our local coaches and our prospective wrestlers.

The high level of available resources, collegiate learning opportunities, and improved avenues of communication systems that have evolved in recent years have provided many tools that leave few excuses for coaches to enter the competitive arena unequipped to meet the needs of each athlete. Some wrestling websites even offer communication forums to allow bulletins and related comments to be discussed and shared about a variety of issues that affect the game and inspire personalized communication about the sport.

We now have the means to find the information that we need to help ensure the success of our wrestlers. Today's numerous media opportunities provide large volumes of access for acquiring information about rankings, results, off-season competitions, and college camps.

We now have the benefit of the information that we need to help inspire a rich sense of ambitious vision that clearly highlights the rewards that are available for those who are willing to make the commitment needed toward achieving success in what this sport has to offer. Many coaches are taking advantage of the wide array of available resources, as they prepare to make a genuine attempt at finding success in the state tournaments across the country.

25

Highlighted Coaches and Contributors: Past and Present

Mark Harris

One example of a high school coach that is making a strong contribution back to his community and leaving his brand on the sport at the state level is Mark Harris. Mark wrestled for Bob Guzzo at NC State University and he is now the Head Coach at Enka High School, his alma mater, near Asheville, North Carolina. He is starting the rebirth of once a well-respected program where he personally won two individual state titles as a high school wrestler.

William Baggett of Enka High School earns himself a defensive pin during the 2004 NCHSAA Regional Tournament quarterfinals match. William was one of eight state qualifiers for Coach Mark Harris that year. (Photograph courtesy of Cathy Starnes, St. Stephens Wrestling.)

Mark Harris, Head Coach at Enka High School, formerly at Fuquay Varina, alongside Gardner Webb Division I qualifier-Daniel Elliot, who was a wrestler for Mark at Fuquay Varina.

Coach Harris has had exceptional early success in his career as a young clinician and motivator. Mark won two NCHSAA Dual State Championships, and two NCHSAA Tournament Championships, as the Head Coach at Fuquay Varina High School in the Southeastern part of Wake County, North Carolina, before returning to the mountains. Coach Harris appears to be building another championship program at Enka. He has helped initiate the development of a club organization to promote wrestling in the Enka/Candler area and in the western part of the state. He is already proving to be a "Pied Piper" with generating a renewed sense of interest and enthusiasm for the sport in his school and community.

Jim Whitmer

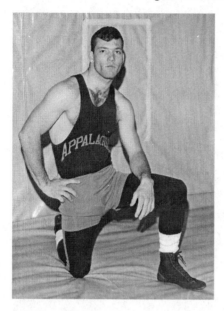

Jim Whitmer, All American Collegiate Wrestler, 1966-67 Wrestling Season at Appalachian State University.

The first successful wrestling tradition was established at Enka by Mark's high school coach, Jim Whitmer. He was one of the historically successful Appalachian State wrestling standouts as a competitor at the University during the mid 1960's. He was an All American as a collegiate wrestler and a member of the Appalachian State "Hall of Fame." After completing a very notable career at ASU he then came to Candler, North Carolina where he led the Enka Jets to numerous wrestling successes for decades. Coach Whitmer enjoyed many years of victories with his powerhouse teams that were developed in the Mountains of North Carolina. He had many athletes that became state champions during his reign.

I had the benefit and the challenge of wrestling and coaching against Coach Whitmer's athletes (Mark Harris included). I was a wrestler at West Henderson High School in Hendersonville, North Carolina in the late 1970's, and I was a coach at the same school, my Alma Mater, from 1986 to 1993. The Enka kids were always fierce competitors and they were tenaciously focused. It was an honor to mix it up with Jim's teams in such an intensive environment, both on the mat as a wrestler, and as a head coach in the same conference with Coach Whitmer during those days. For many years Jim's wrestling portrait hung in the Trophy case in Varsity Gym, on the ASU campus. The portrait is now gone, but the impact he had as an athlete at ASU, and the overwhelming difference he made in the lives of numerous young men, for many years around the Hominy Valley area of Buncombe County, will never be forgotten.

Jim Whitmer coaching at Enka High School.

Herb Singerman

ASU Team 1969 Herb Singerman, front-center, and Paul Mance, back-center.

Around the time that Jim Whitmer was about to finish his successful wrestling career at Appalachian State University, a young man from Montreal had just completed his shot at the 1968 Summer Olympic Games, as a competitor for the Canadian Olympic Wrestling Team. His name was Herb Singerman. In the spring of 1968 Coach Gabriel had contacted Herb about coming to ASU to wrestle during the fall semester of that year where he was to begin a collegiate career for the Mountaineers. But, because of his Olympic opportunity, he had to wait to arrive until what was then called the winter quarter at ASU. Herb rode a bus for a day and a half from Montreal, Canada to New York, and then to Hickory, North Carolina. He then made a final bus trip up the Mountain to Boone, NC, where Coach Gabriel picked him up from the station.

Coach Gabriel then took Herb and went directly to the ASU cafeteria where they found Jim Whitmer, and together they were escorted to the wrestling room at the university for a sparring session between the two exceptional competitors. After speaking with both men (Jim and Herb) about that unique sparring session, during conversations in the summer of the year 2005, each one could not have been more complimentary about the other's previous skill level in that contest. They both had vivid memories of Coach Gabriel's version of giving Herb an orientation to the campus and to the program.

Herb wrestled on the team along with Paul Mance at a time when something special was going on in Boone, and in North Carolina wrestling. A large nucleus of well skilled athletes and coaches-to-be had begun descending on the ASU Program for a number of years that would forever impact the future of many young lives in the years to come.

Herb became one of the first wrestlers at ASU to qualify for the NCAA Tournament. It was at about that time when the ASU program had left the NAIA Division of competition to move up to the next level. After a successful wrestling career in Boone, Herb took a coaching job at Reidsville High School in Rockingham County, NC. He later came back to Boone as a graduate assistant and assistant college coach at ASU for two years.

Coach Singerman has spent much of the last 35 years successfully teaching, coaching, and officiating the sport that he loves. Most of his on-going contribution to the young people in wrestling has been done in the Asheville area of North Carolina. He did stints as the head coach at Asheville High School, and North Buncombe, before finishing his career after nine consecutive years as the head coach at AC Reynolds High School in the Fairview area of Buncombe County. Herb was able to guide four young men to individual state wrestling titles during his efforts as a head coach. And, he made an effective contribution as a preferred official in the mountains for many years.

NCHSAA Sectional Semi-final, Official Herb Singerman, Wrestler-Darrell McDowell, white headgear, in a bloody match vs. Larry Martin-state qualifier for Enka High School.

John Mark Bentley

Another promising young coach that is making an early impact in this sport, and is beginning to be recognized as a serious threat to contend on the statewide scene is John-Mark Bentley. He was recently hired as the head wrestling coach at Watauga High School in the town of Boone, North Carolina. He accepted the position with the Pioneers two years ago and he has already made his presence well known with the admirable performance of a number of his wrestlers that qualified and competed in the 2005 North Carolina Individual State Tournament.

Coach Bentley was a four-time NCHSAA State Champion during his scholastic career at the neighboring Avery County High School, located in an area of the state not too far from Grandfather Mountain. He was a former participant in the Strong and Courageous Program that was mentioned in the previous chapters. John-Mark found success and gained effective experience at the university level as a competitor at the University of North Carolina at Chapel Hill, where he wrestled three years for the Tarheels. And he participated one year as a member of the Oklahoma State wrestling team where he had the advantage of wrestling for the well renowned and internationally respected coach John Smith.

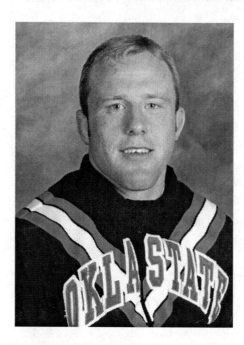

John Mark Bentley, Head Coach at Watauga High School in Boone, North Carolina.

Coach Bentley has been humble and gracious with his progressive instruction as a high school head coach. He is already well on his way to ensuring the success of his own team while instructing other kids at the Appalachian State Camp with his enthusiastic and motivated sense of contribution. It appears that he has probably only begun to reap the benefits of the knowledge that he has obtained from his intensive and exceptional experiences. And, he appears to be generous with his efforts to share what he has learned with others in the game.

As mentioned previously, much of the foundation for establishing solid growth and ensuring stable numbers of scholastic coaches that are willing to stay in the southeast and make a wholesale contribution to improving wrestling in the area are generated by the conscientious schools of wrestling like Appalachian State University and the University of North Carolina at Pembroke.

Greg Frey

Greg Frey, Head Coach at Morehead High School in Eden, North Carolina at the 1999 Dual State Championships in a 41 to 24 victory over Tuscola High School from Waynesville, North Carolina.

Greg wrestled at the University of North Carolina at Pembroke. Pembroke is a small college that is a part of the North Carolina University System. The school is located in the Southeastern part of the state near Fayetteville. Coach Frey wrestled at Fayetteville Seventy-First High School and was a tough wrestler at the college level, wrestling in the competitive ranks of the NAIA Division for the Pembroke Braves, under the direction of Mike Olson. Coach Olson was a very successful and stubbornly competitive, head coach who had an inescapable impact on anyone he ever instructed. And he is highlighted in the nation's wrestling record books for his numerous team victories. Pembroke is located in Robeson County and has a strong history of success in wrestling. And, it is still very competitive under the direction of Head Coach P. J. Smith.

Greg Frey, Head Coach at Morehead Eden High School, and Mike Olson, then Head Coach at Pembroke State University, as Greg committed to wrestling for the Pembroke Braves.

After leaving Pembroke, Greg Frey landed the job as the head coach at Morehead High School, in Eden, North Carolina. His long and effective reign with the Panthers has reflected the same threatening posture of physical toughness, and the refined level of skill that was expected by Coach Olson at Pembroke State, and it is clearly evidenced in the outstanding performances of the Panther wrestling teams.

Coach Frey has made Morehead High School a successful and well-respected part of the amateur wrestling scene in

North Carolina. His outstanding coaching methods have secured a total of four NCHSAA Dual State Championships and two NCHSAA Tournament Championships during his tenure as the Panthers head coach. Greg is another example of an excellent coach who cares deeply about his wrestling athletes. During his successful time as the head coach at Morehead in Rockingham County, North Carolina, he has provided quality instruction and developed many motivated groups of tough competitors. His on-going efforts to host exceptional tournaments and ensure a competitive environment at the Eden site have helped to promote the quality of the sport. His contributions have been an important part of the overall growth of amateur wrestling in this state.

Evan Johnson of Morehead High School being hoisted and honored by his teammates in an upset victory against a reigning state champion Tripp Rogers from East Gaston High School that ultimately decided the NCHSAA Dual State Championship match on February 7, 2003 with Morehead's 31 to 26 victory over East Gaston. Johnson's victory over Rogers may be the most significant win in the wrestling history of the school. Photograph by Robert Ross/Eden Daily News

Darrell McDowell

Darrell McDowell, Freshman at Pembroke State University in 1979.

As a college student, I had the benefit and the advantage of wrestling at both Pembroke State for Mike Olson (the toughest man I've ever known) and at Appalachian State for Paul Mance, who is also a staunch competitor. The experiences that are gained while wrestling at the university level can have a very positive affect on the overall formula for achieving success as a high school coach at the state-wide level of competition. This intensive exposure helps drive the process for improving the quality of wrestling throughout the region and ensures continued advancements in the skill level of our athletes across the nation.

I began my career as a head coach at Madison/Mayodan High School at the age of twenty-two in Rockingham

County, North Carolina. This was at a time in history when you could still wrestle matches in front of the student body, during the school day. Greg Frey and I alternated sites each of the years that I worked as the coach at Madison/ Mayodan. There were some fierce matches with all of the emotion generated by the big crowds of students. It was a lot of fun for the coaches and the kids.

After three years, I moved back to the Western part of the state to my alma mater. At that time West Henderson had just gone through a five-year drought of sending no wrestlers to the State Tournament. I was fortunate to have coached five wrestlers to Individual State Champion titles during my stay as the Head Coach at West Henderson High School during the late 1980's and early 1990's.

The success that we enjoyed at West Henderson was established just before I traded my heart for a career in school administration. One of my most tenacious NC State Champions was a young man named Kyle Kuykendall that wrestled for me at West Henderson. Kyle went on in his college career to become a Southern Conference Champion. Like me, he also wrestled for Coach Mance at Appalachian State. I, and many others, owe a great debt of experience and opportunity to the collegiate leaders in this sport who have chosen to spend their lives coaching at the intensive university level of competition. Their contribution of effective instruction has had a progressive impact on the growth of amateur wrestling in this part of the country.

Kyle Kuykendall, NC State Champion 1990 at West Henderson High School and Southern Conference Champion at Appalachian State University.

John Welborn

John Welborn, Boone native and Head Coach at East Carolina University.

J.W. Welborn was an outstanding Appalachian State University wrestler that was also a competitor on several of Steve Gabriel's Dynasty of High School teams during his scholastic career. After his association with ASU he then settled into an unprecedented career of victories as the head wrestling coach at East Carolina University. Coach Welborn was, at one time, a team member alongside Bill Mayhew and Mike Raybon at ASU before traveling down the mountain to the Eastern part of the state in Greenville where he established a span of victories in Wresting at ECU that dominated the college wrestling scene in North Carolina, and in much of the surrounding area for many years.

Many of his former wrestlers speak very highly of this man and they are still very enthusiastic about proclaiming the merits of his coaching style. Most suggest that he motivated them to superior levels of performance, in part because of their dedication to his clear vision of expectations. They were intense and enthusiastic because they felt he cared deeply about each one of them as an individual.

One of the great tragedies for the sport of wrestling occurred when John Welborn retired his position as the head wrestling coach for the Pirates, and in a few short years the wrestling program was dropped from the Athletic Department at ECU. This, along with the decision to drop the program at Clemson University, definitely injured the prospective opportunities that were available for wrestlers in the Southeastern United States.

But all was not lost when Welborn left the wrestling program at ECU. He had created a legacy for himself and the sport that reinforced the fraternal order and the culture that he had created in the game. His efforts produced coaches who carried on the winning tradition that he had drilled into the dreams and the futures of his many protégés as they settled into their own successful situations.

As a tribute to his outstanding career, Coach Welborn has been recognized with a Lifetime Service Award as he was inducted into the National Wrestling Hall of Fame in Stillwater, Oklahoma.

Milt Sherman

Milt Sherman, former ECU Wrestling Stand-out and Head Coach at D.H. Conley High School.

One outstanding college competitor from ECU, who wrestled for Coach Welborn, went on to become the head coach at D.H. Conley High School, also in the Eastern part of North Carolina. Milt Sherman had a very successful college career at ECU and went on to assemble many dominating teams during his long reign at D.H. Conley, winning an Individual State Tournament Championship in 1995.

Coach Sherman's young men were well-equipped with a consistent and masterful combination of technical expertise and motivated by a relentless approach to competing at the highest level. His wrestlers were always in the mix of potential champions at the State Tournament. They were well-prepared and difficult to defend with a very complete and effective arsenal of tools that were used to challenge opponents in each and every match.

Head Coach Milt Sherman and his 1995 D.H. Conley NCHSAA State Tournament Championship Team.

Another contribution of Milt Sherman includes the publication of a number of wrestling articles that he wrote for a wide variety of sports magazines. His articulation of strategies and his contribution of technical advice have been effective for a widespread audience of coaches and wrestling enthusiasts all over the nation. He has expansive knowledge of the details of the game, and he has made it his personal ambition to ensure the promotion and the success of amateur wrestling in North Carolina.

Coach Sherman has also been recognized with a Lifetime Service Award and inducted into the National Wrestling Hall of Fame in Stillwater, Oklahoma.

Wally Burke

Wally Burke, Head Coach at High Point Andrews with 3x place winner-Sam "Squirt" McKiver. Coach Burke was also recently recognized for his efforts with a Lifetime Service Award and inducted into the National Wrestling Hall of Fame in Stillwater, Oklahoma.

Wally Burke, at High Point Andrews High School, assembled one of the most impressive displays of a disciplined and aggressive approach to winning state championships, in North Carolina wrestling history. Like

Coach Sherman at D.H. Conley, Coach Burke hails from the Fairfax, Virginia area. He attended Elon College after graduating from W.T. Woodson High School and he wrestled for a short time at Elon before he started his coaching career.

I had the opportunity to have several of my wrestlers face his athletes at the State Tournament during the prime years of Coach Burke's successful string of victories as his teams won five consecutive Individual State Tournament Championships from 1987 through 1991. He also won a North Carolina State Tournament Championship at Andrews in 1981 and another Individual State Championship as the Head Coach at Southern Alamance High School in 1975 prior to his dominating reign at T.W Andrews in High Point, NC.

As impressive as were the individual performances of his very athletic and well-equipped competitors was the level of participation and the focused approach that was used to motivate a team concept during each match. The enthusiastic chants and the contagious sense of motivated vocal support provided to each team member clearly changed the climate of the arena and reinforced an expectation of fierce competition by all members of his team and by much of his other fan support. When the "Red Raiders" took the mat, they often brought with them an ominous presence of understood respect and intimidation that accompanied even some of their lesser-equipped participants.

High Point Andrews State Champion Team. This team had seven finalists and four state champions on the same squad.

Coach Burke appeared to have established strong relationships and expectations with the wrestlers in his program that resulted in successful results and numerous rewards for those that were willing to endure his disciplined approach to winning championships. His athletes always displayed a consistent element of endurance, perseverance, and fundamental effectiveness in their performance that resulted in tremendous success. His approach to the game provided many opportunities for his wrestlers and created a program that cannot be viewed as anything less than a respected dynasty that will not be soon forgotten in the memories of North Carolina wrestling.

Bill Mayhew

Bill Mayhew has made a tremendous contribution to the sport of wrestling and to the game of football, in North Carolina. He was the head wrestling and football coach at Troutman High School in the early days of his coaching career, and then he secured the job at South Iredell High School, in Iredell County near Statesville, North Carolina.

Bill is a soft-spoken disciplinarian who has been able to balance his athletic programs to their maximum potential. His athletes appear to be great sportsman and intensely driven to excel. The formula that Coach Mayhew prescribed for his wrestlers secured his team a North Carolina State Tournament Championship Title in 1986. The championship atmosphere at that event was even further enhanced and highlighted by the fact that Coach Mayhew was able to embrace the personal satisfaction and the great sense of pride associated with coaching his own son at that event. Mitch Mayhew earned himself a State Championship Title at his weight class in 1986, as his father coached he and his teammates to the NC State Tournament Title.

Father and Son Photo: Bill and Mitch Mayhew at South Iredell High School.

Coach Mayhew also holds the distinction and the honor of being recognized for recording the most wins that have ever been accrued by any wrestling coach in the history of North Carolina. And, what may be most impressive about his ability to influence young people is that his success as a head football coach closely rivals his accomplishments in wrestling.

Coach Mayhew appears to have a universal appeal that has paid great dividends to his athletes and his community. He is another Appalachian State Alumnus that came down the mountain and established an effective career of service and success. Before leaving ASU as a student, Bill Mayhew accumulated four Varsity Lettermen Awards in football and four more in wrestling. And, he bore through his last two years as a Mountaineer wrestler with an undefeated record in regular season competition.

Coach Mayhew is also a recipient of the Lifetime Service Award in Wrestling and he was inducted into the National Wrestling Hall of Fame in Stillwater, Oklahoma.

Bill Mayhew college wrestling picture from Appalachian State University Wrestling Team, 1963.

Jerry Winterton

Coach Jerry Winterton of Cary High School.
Photo by David Maney II, CHS Sports Information Director.

I cannot close the door on these superlative and highlighted coaches in North Carolina in good conscience without recognizing the significant accomplishments of Jerry Winterton at Cary High School near Raleigh. Cary has won more NCHSAA State Championships than any other school in recent wrestling history.

In 1977, John Sanderson was the head coach at Cary and led the Imps to their first Individual State Championship Tournament victory. Winterton followed Sanderson's period of leadership beginning in 1981, and has continued this winning tradition with an enormous level of success. He is very complimentary of what Sanderson had begun to establish at the school in terms of wins, and the emphasis that had been placed on instilling and demanding a "class act" with regard to professionalism and maturity from the Cary athletes.

Coach Winterton is still the head coach at Cary High School and his accumulation of accomplishments are almost endless. He has won a total of seven State Individual Tournament Championships and five Dual State Championships. He is also highly recognized for having won more individual tournaments than any other coach in the nation. His total number of tournament victories is <u>135</u>. That's <u>four</u> more than <u>Jim Husk</u> from Florida. Jerry is enjoying a phenomenal career as the head coach at Cary.

Like Bill Mayhew at South Iredell, Coach Winterton was blessed with the opportunity and the privilege of coaching his own son to a personal individual state championship title as a competitor for the Imps. As mentioned throughout this book, there is a fraternal order associated with this game that often encourages the kind of work ethic and persistence that ensures a level of inclusion in the sport among families and dedicated team members as they develop a love for the wrestling game. Although Coach Winterton is quick to suggest that coaching your own child can be a tumultuous task with all of the pressures that accompany an effort to be a parent and a coach all rolled into one, he could not be happier about what it has meant to him to have had that experience.

His son Logan got a late start in the game as an eighth grade student, when compared to many individuals who begin competing at a much younger age. But he quickly made up for his lack of early experience by winning a state title, and now he looks forward to a career at the college level of participation at Appalachian State University with Coach Mance in Boone.

Coach Winterton acknowledges that he, like coach Mayhew, is very proud of his son's efforts and his team's exceptional history of success. Like Wally Burke at High Point Andrews, Coach Winterton has created a highly recognized wrestling dynasty that is well-respected in this state and across the nation. He is in high demand as a technician and a clinician in the sport. He has extreme expectations for a level of personal class and intensive performance among his athletes. And, there is much evidence to confirm the results of his disciplined efforts as the head coach at Cary. Coach Winteron's intensive expectations are clearly reflected in the level of success exhibited on the mat, and in the way his wrestlers behave as young men.

Coach Winterton was also recently inducted into the National Wrestling Hall of Fame in Stillwater, Oklahoma with a Lifetime Service Award.

Father and son Photo: Jerry Winterton as he coached his son, Logan.

Other Coaches

Rex Wells and Jim Whitmer coaching together in a West Henderson vs. Enka match, in the early 1990's. Kris Kirtley is the West Henderson wrestler on the mat. Kris was a 3rd place and a 4th place finisher in the NCHSAA State Championship in his junior and senior year.

There is a long list of other extremely successful high school coaches in the state of North Carolina, far too many to mention here. But the following list is an accumulation of individuals who I knew and was able to witness their inspired efforts to change the lives of numerous young men. This list can in no way include all of the outstanding coaches in the state, because of my limited exposure to certain classifications and demographics. I apologize for any that I did not get to meet or failed to recognize in this document.

It was a great pleasure and an honor to have been fortunate enough to have met and communicated with many outstanding individuals during my travels as a high school coach. But the following group, along with many that you will be able to view on the attached list of State Championships Results that is a part of this book, has truly helped to mold the progress of our sport.

The following are just a few of the great coaches that I once knew and learned valuable ideas from during the time that I enjoyed as a coach in North Carolina: Paul Crouse formerly at Allegany, Greg Hardin at Eastern Randolph, Steve Atwood formerly at Mitchell and Tuscola, Rex Wells formerly at Brevard and Asheville, Steve Moffit formerly at Kings Mountain, Scott Goins at East Gaston, Jeff Smith at West Henderson, Barry Cannon at East Henderson, Rick Williams formerly at South Stokes, Mike Stanbridge formerly at Cape Fear, Herman Norman formerly at Starmount and Wilkes Community College, Harold Smith formerly at Trinity, High Point Central and RJ Reynolds, David Rothwell at Statesville, and John Sanderson who was at Cary before working as a head coach and school administrator at both Pisgah and Tuscola High Schools in Haywood County, in the Western part of the state. Richie Houston formerly at Cherokee, now at Madison High in GA, Larry Carpenter formerly at St. Stephens, Heang Uy at North Henderson and Jason Joyce at Apple Valley Middle School.

Other notable programs that have moved to the competitive forefront in recent years would have to include Ronnie Sigmon and Forest Blake with their co-coaching arrangement at Bandys High School, Freddie Little at Chatham Central, and it would be very difficult to ignore the impressive efforts and results on the part of Bob Shriner and his staff of coaches at Orange High School. And then Ragsdale High School continues their perennial success under the direction of Andy Chappell contributing state championship levels of performance.

One other successful coach that I gained a great deal of respect for as I observed and competed against his teams, when he made his way up to the Asheville area for the early season tournament at TC Roberson High School, was Jim Barnes. His athletes were always very impressive. His outstanding teams won numerous State Championships for many years at Rock Hill High School in South Carolina. Coach Barnes has now moved to North Carolina where he coaches the wrestling team at E.E. Waddell High School in Charlotte, North Carolina. He brings with him a wealth of knowledge and experience.

Again, these are just a very few on a list of very passionate individuals with impressive careers and resumes who have approached the game with admirable and effective efforts. I have been very fortunate to have known them, and been able to compete with most of there teams in an arena of performance that has enabled me to assess the depth of their accomplishments in the sport. Their hard work and attention to detailed instruction, along with the efforts of many others, have clearly helped move amateur wrestling in North Carolina toward a consistent path of improvement.

Hall of Fame

Many of the individuals that have been mentioned in this book are certainly worthy of a high level of hard-earned and well-deserved recognition. Just recently, a number of the coaches and others involved in this sport from North Carolina were awarded with a most high honor for their service and accomplishments in amateur wrestling. Each of the following individuals was inducted into the National Wrestling Hall of Fame and received Lifetime Service Awards for their contributions to the sport:

National Wrestling Hall of Fame
Stillwater, Oklahoma

Lifetime Service Award Winners

Wally Burke – Coach – Southern Alamance and High Point Andrews
High Schools
Jerry Daniels - Coach – North Carolina State University
Kathy Dick – Contributor
Richard Steve Gabriel – Coach – Appalachian High School, Boone, NC
Bill Harvey – Coach – Duke University
Joe Jones – Official – Official
Bill Kemp – Coach – Goldsboro High School
Bill Lam – Coach – University of North Carolina at Chapel Hill
Bob Mauldin – Mat News
Bill Mayhew – Coach-South Iredell High School
Frank Rader – USA Wrestling
Mike Raybon – Coach – Ragsdale High School
Milt Sherman – Coach – D.H. Conley High School
John Welborn – Coach – East Carolina University
Jerry Winterton – Coach – Cary High School

National Wrestling Hall of Fame
Medal of Courage

Dock Kelly

Dock Kelly will be eternally recognized in the Hall of Fame
in Stillwater, Oklahoma for receiving the Medal of Courage
Award. He was inducted into the Hall of Fame for his
competitive spirit and the tremendous success he enjoyed,
even against very extreme odds. He was born with a birth
defect that left him with one leg that had to be removed just

below the knee. And one of his hands is fingerless. He participated in the wrestling program at Southern Pines High School near Pinehurst, North Carolina, where he was awarded Wrestler of the Year during his senior year in his conference. He wrestled in college at the University of North Carolina at Greensboro where he qualified for the NCAA Division I Nationals. He was also able to win the Mountaineer Open Tournament at Appalachian State University where he put together five victories in sequence to walk away with a Championship medal in that event. (National Wrestling Hall of Fame Website-http: //www.wrestlinghalloffame.org, 2005).

Dock was recently named the head wrestling coach at Anderson College, located in the Upper South Carolina area, after serving four years as an assistant coach at his alma mater at the University of North Carolina at Greensboro.

North Carolina Four-Time State Champions

Mike Kendall – Albemarle High School 1991
Collegiate – University of North Carolina at Chapel Hill
John Mark Bentley – Avery High School 1997
Collegiate - UNC and Oklahoma State University
Drew Forshey – Saint Stephens High School 2003
Collegiate – University of North Carolina at Chapel Hill
Dusty McKinney – East Gaston High School 2004
Collegiate – George Mason University

North Carolina State Championship Wrestling Results:

All NCHSAA Results were provided as a courtesy of the North Carolina High School Athletic Association located in Chapel Hill, North Carolina.

NCHSAA STATE TOURNAMENT CHAMPIONS

OPEN

YEAR SITE CHAMPION COACH POINTS

MOST OUTSTANDING WRESTLER

1931 UNC-Chapel Hill Durham William Uzzell 22
1932 UNC-Chapel Hill Durham William Uzzell 47
1933 UNC-Chapel Hill Greensboro Tom Jenrette 40
1934 UNC-Chapel Hill Barium Springs 34
1935 UNC-Chapel Hill Barium Springs 33
1936 UNC-Chapel Hill Barium Springs Buck Jackins 41
1937 UNC-Chapel Hill Barium Springs 50
1938 UNC-Chapel Hill Barium Springs 44
1939 UNC-Chapel Hill Greensboro Tom Jenrette 53
1940 UNC-Chapel Hill Durham B.J. Stewart 26
1941 UNC-Chapel Hill Barium Springs 26
Greensboro Tom Jenrette 26
1942 UNC-Chapel Hill Salisbury J.H. Nettles 24
1947 High Point High Point Bob Sappenfield 18
1948 High Point High Point Bob Sappenfield
1949 High Point High Point Bob Sappenfield
1952 High Point High Point Leon Ellis 51
1953 High Point High Point Leon Ellis 55
1954 High Point High Point 55
1955 High Point High Point George Gilley 89
1956 Greensboro Greensboro Lody Glenn 103
1957 Burlington Boone Appalachian Steve Gabriel 92
1958 Burlington Boone Appalachian Steve Gabriel 109 Bill Cook,
Boone Appalachian
1959 Goldsboro Boone Appalachian Steve Gabriel 102 Doug Carson,
Boone Appalachian (123)
Irvin Hales, Goldsboro (115)
1960 Greensboro Boone Appalachian Steve Gabriel 119 Paul Stork,

Myers Park (165)

1961 High Point Thomasville Harpo Withers 56 Doug Carson, Boone Appalachian (127)

1962 High Point Boone Appalachian Steve Gabriel 69 Bill Cooke, Boone Appalachian (133)

1963 High Point Boone Appalachian Steve Gabriel 79 Joy Loy, Burlington (145)

1964 Boone Appalachian Boone Appalachian Steve Gabriel 85 Gary Brown, Boone Appalachian (154)

1965 Boone Appalachian Boone Appalachian Steve Gabriel 83 Dickie Bryant, West Mecklenburg (95)

1966 Salisbury Goldsboro William Kemp 51

1967 Reynolds Grimsley Kent Umberger 50 Curtis Weaver, Grimsley (133)

1968 Parkland Myers Park John Peel 45 Eric Herbert, Cary (136)

1969 Parkland Reidsville Charlie Rayburn 43 Allen Barnett, North Mecklenburg (138)

1970 Parkland Page 39 John Starkey, Olympic (126)

1971 Parkland Page 43 Ferrell Snotherly, Page (heavyweight)

1972 Parkland Ragsdale Mike Raybon 47.5 John Blackmon, East Mecklenburg (122)

1973 Parkland Brevard Rex Wells 40.5 Billy Rumley, Reidsville (135)

1974 Parkland Goldsboro William Kemp 46.5 Eddie Foster, Southern Alamance (105)

1975 Parkland Southern Alamance Wally Burke 73.5 Benny Brooks, Southern Alamance (141)

1976 Parkland Grimsley Dennis Barbour 69 Bobby Joyner, NW Guilford (155)

1977 Parkland Cary John Sanderson 87.5 Barry Armstrong, Cary (141)

1978 Parkland Ragsdale Mike Raybon 63.5 Chuck Gordon, Kings Mountain (hwt)

1979 Parkland South Stokes Bob Scheib 55.5 Ron Manns, South Stokes (141)

1980 Parkland Trinity Harold Smith 51 Gary Harris, D.H. Conley (115)

1981 Parkland T.W. Andrews Wally Burke 66.5 Randy Lowery, Brevard (135)

1982 Parkland Ragsdale Mike Raybon 55 Mike Long, D.H. Conley (188)

1983 Parkland Sanderson Dale Warren 56.5 Jon Bullins, Madison-Mayodan (hwt)

1984 Parkland Cape Fear Mike Stanbridge 84.5 Mike Stokes, Tarboro (122)

1985 Parkland Brevard Rex Wells 87 Tim Ellenburger, Brevard (101)

1986 Parkland South Iredell Bill Mayhew 65.5 Dexter Jones, Hoke County (129

PLAY WENT TO CLASS A/AA, AAA, AND AAA IN 1987

CLASS AAAA
YEAR SITE CHAMPION COACH POINTS MOST OUTSTANDING WRESTLER

1987 East Forsyth Cary Jerry Winterton 98.5 David Gragson, Independence (138)

1988 East Forsyth Cary Jerry Winterton 131.5 Shawn Phillips, East Burke (135)

1989 East Forsyth Cary Jerry Winterton 88.5 Pat King, Cary (130)

1990 Grimsley Jordan Randy Rogers 82 Heath Wilson, Cape Fear (152)

1991 Greensboro ColiseumEast Gaston Doug Smith 85.5 Jared Ezzell, Jordan (125)

1992 Greensboro ColiseumE.A. Laney Alan Sewell 78 Andrew Humphrey, E.A. Laney (171)

1993 Greensboro ColiseumAnson County Jack Southern 82.5 Bob Mobley, Apex (103)

1994 Greensboro ColiseumRiverside Jim Key 138 C.C. Fisher, Durham Riverside (125)

1995 Independence Arena Davie County Buddy Lowery 121 Dwane Cason, E.E. Smith (189)

1996 Independence Arena Anson County Steve Emory 96.5 Deuce Harris, Durham Riverside (140)

1997 Independence Arena Cary Jerry Winterton 122.5 Ronnie Dunbar, Raleigh Broughton(119)

1998 Independence Arena Seventy-First David Culbreth 144 Ben Annas, Northwest Guilford (171)

1999 Independence Arena Seventy-First David Culbreth 191 Kevin Stanley, W.Forest-Rolesville(171)

2000 Independence Arena Cary Jerry Winterton 143 Tyrone Hodge, Orange (119)

2001 Independence Arena Mount Tabor Jason Hooker 115 Tyrone Hodge, Orange (119)

2002 Cricket Arena Riverside Walt Tolarchyk 162 Garrett Atkinson, Watauga (145)

2003 Lawrence Joel Cary Jerry Winterton 176.5 Raymond Jordan, New Bern (160)

2004 Lawrence Joel Riverside Walt Tolarchyk 159.5 Raymond Jordan, New Bern (171)

2005 Lawrence Joel Cary Jerry Winterton 126 Jake Smith, Jack Britt (145)

CLASS AAA
YEAR SITE CHAMPION COACH POINTS MOST OUTSTANDING WRESTLER

1987 UNC-Chapel Hill T.W. Andrews Wally Burke 139 Bernard Terry, T.W. Andrews (105)

1988 UNC-Chapel Hill T.W. Andrews Wally Burke 105.5 Larry Harris, Washington (189)

1989 Grimsley T.W. Andrews Wally Burke 84 Brent David, T.W. Andrews (189)

1990 T.W. Andrews T.W. Andrews Wally Burke 86.5 Carlos Hough, T.W. Andrews (103)

1991 Greensboro Coliseum T.W. Andrews Wally Burke 148 Kenny Bailey, Statesville (112)

1992 Greensboro ColiseumStatesville David Rothwell 80.5 Perry Long, Sun Valley (171)

Sun Valley Mike Webb 80.5

1993 Greensboro Coliseum Eastern Randolph Greg Hardin 79.5 Chris Bloech, NW Guilford (160)

1994 Greensboro Coliseum High Point Central Andy Chappell 69 Ritz Etter, A.L. Brown (130)

1995 Independence Arena D.H. Conley Milt Sherman 68 Conan Manka, Eastern Randolph (275)

1996 Independence Arena Havelock David Siler 93.5 Clay Reynolds, High Point Central (125)

1997 Independence Arena Havelock David Siler 67.0 Russ Chesson, Washington (103)

Parkland Greg Atwood 67.0

Ragsdale Andy Chappell 67.0

1998 Independence Arena J.M.Morehead Greg Frey 87.5 Julius Curry, Kings Mountain (275)

1999 Independence Arena J.M.Morehead Greg Frey 114 Jared Raymond, Morehead (119)

2000 Independence Arena Fuquay-Varina Mark Harris 98 Josh Allman, Northwest Cabarrus (145)

2001 Independence Arena Havelock David Siler 84 Curry Pickard, Eden Morehead (125)

Fuquay-Varina Mark Harris 84

2002 Cricket Arena East Gaston Scott Goins 100 Dusty McKinney, East Gaston (112)

2003 Lawrence Joel East Gaston Scott Goins 133 Drew Forshey, St. Stephens (125)

2004 Lawrence Joel East Gaston Scott Goins 118.5 Dusty McKinney, East Gaston (125)

2005 Lawrence Joel Ragsdale Andy Chappell 97 Kyle Kanaga, Ragsdale (125)

CLASS A/AA

YEAR SITE CHAMPION COACH POINTS MOST OUTSTANDING WRESTLER

1987 Ledford Piedmont Tim Blair 89.5 Mark Royall, Starmount (158)
1988 Ledford Mitchell Steve Atwood 118.5 Renee Taylor, Mitchell (130)
1989 Ledford Alleghany Jim Smith 107.5 Chris Moses, Newton-Conover (130)
1990 Ledford Mitchell Steve Atwood 107.5 Mike Kendall, Albemarle (119)
1991 Greensboro Coliseum Thomasville J.C. Young 79.5 Mike Kendall, Albemarle (130)
1992 Greensboro Coliseum Albemarle Wes Eidson 98 Phil Carlton, Mount Pleasant (119)
1993 Greensboro Coliseum Dixon Homer Spring 75 James Orr, Robbinsville (112)
1994 Greensboro Coliseum North Henderson Barry Bonnett 102.5 James Short, North Henderson (189)
1995 Independence Arena Eastern Guilford Robbie Harris 68 Earl Roland, Ashe Central (160)
1996 Independence Arena East Henderson Michael Ecker 89 Steven Short, North Henderson (140)
1997 Independence Arena Alleghany Paul Crouse 124.5 JohnMark Bentley, Avery Co (130)
1998 Independence Arena Alleghany Paul Crouse 127 James Lewis, C.D.Owen (215)
1999 Independence Arena Eastern Randolph Greg Hardin 92.5 Justin Parlier, Alleghany (145)
2000 Independence Arena Eastern Randolph Greg Hardin 104 Jordan

Binder, Currituck (125)

2001 Independence Arena Southern Vance Tom McArdle 117.5 Patrick Lewis, Southern Vance (135)

2002 Cricket Arena Southern Vance Tom McArdle 135.5 Austin Mikael, Ashe County (160)

2003 Lawrence Joel T.W. Andrews Ron Crawford 133.5 Elliott Darden, T.W. Andrews (125)

2004 Lawrence Joel Bandys Forrest Blake 108 Chris Bullins, McMichael (160)

Brevard Vernon Bryson 108

2005 Lawrence Joel Bandys Forrest Blake 168.5 Eddie Sawyer, Currituck (145)

NCHSAA WRESTLING CHAMPIONS

STATE DUAL MEET CHAMPIONSHIPS

AAAA
YEAR CHAMPION RUNNER-UP

1990 East Gaston 35 Durham Jordan 24

1991 East Gaston 40 Cary 15

1992 East Gaston 30 Orange 25

1993 Cary 26 Davie County 22

1994 Davie County 31 Durham Riverside 28

1995 Durham Riverside 33 Davie County 31

1996 Cary 28 Durham Riverside 26

1997 Cary 33 Orange 29

1998 Cary 35 Independence 34

1999 Fayetteville Seventy-First 50 Davie County 13

2000 Fayetteville Seventy-First 40 Davie County 25

2001 W-Salem Mount Tabor 37 Cary 18

2002 Durham Riverside 40 Cary 26

2003 Durham Riverside 38 Cary 30
2004 Durham Riverside 35 Cary 28
2005 Cary 34 Davie County 32

AAA
YEAR CHAMPION RUNNER-UP

1990 T.W. Andrews 51 Kings Mountain 10
1991 T.W. Andrews 38 Central Davidson 13
1992 T.W. Andrews 34 Statesville 27
1993 Sun Valley 50 Northwest Guilford 16
1994 High Point Central 34 West Carteret 29
1995 Winston-Salem Parkland 27 Ragsdale 25
1996 Winston-Salem Parkland 40 Havelock 25
1997 Havelock 48 Winston-Salem Parkland 28
1998 Eden John M. Morehead 32 North Gaston 28
1999 Eden John M. Morehead 40 Waynesville Tuscola 24
2000 Fuquay-Varina 36 Waynesville Tuscola 28
2001 Fuquay-Varina 46 Hickory St. Stephens 11
2002 Eden John M. Morehead 34 Hickory St. Stephens 26
2003 Eden John M. Morehead 31 East Gaston 26
2004 Jamestown Ragsdale 40 Eden John M. Morehead 25
2005 Orange 30 East Gaston 28

A/AA
YEAR CHAMPION RUNNER-UP

1990 Dixon 38 Mitchell County 28
1991 Albemarle 40 Mount Pleasant 23
1992 Dixon 30 Avery County 25
1993 East Davidson 27 Ashe Central 26
1994 Dixon 36 North Henderson 28
1995 East Davidson 28 Mount Pleasant 25
1996 West Henderson 28 East Davidson 26

1997 Alleghany 30 East Davidson 27
1998 North Wilkes 40 East Davidson 32
1999 Alleghany 37 Currituck 36
2000 West Lincoln 36 Southern Vance 23
2001 Canton Pisgah 31 Southern Vance 30

AA
YEAR CHAMPION RUNNER-UP

2002 Southern Vance 36 Canton Pisgah 34
2003 Southern Vance 34 Brevard 30
2004 McMichael 45 West Stokes 16
2005 Bandys 41 Croatan 15

A
YEAR CHAMPION RUNNER-UP

2002 Alleghany 48 South Davidson 18
2003 South Davidson 37 Alleghany 27
2004 Elkin 34 West Davidson 32
2005 Chatham Central 43 East Surry 36

NCHSAA WRESTLING CHAMPIONS

Courtesy of the North Carolina High School Athletic Association, Chapel Hill, North Carolina

STATE DUAL MEET CHAMPIONSHIPS

AAAA
YEAR CHAMPION RUNNER-UP

1990 East Gaston 35 Durham Jordan 24
1991 East Gaston 40 Cary 15
1992 East Gaston 30 Orange 25
1993 Cary 26 Davie County 22
1994 Davie County 31 Durham Riverside 28
1995 Durham Riverside 33 Davie County 31
1996 Cary 28 Durham Riverside 26
1997 Cary 33 Orange 29
1998 Cary 35 Independence 34
1999 Fayetteville Seventy-First 50 Davie County 13
2000 Fayetteville Seventy-First 40 Davie County 25
2001 W-Salem Mount Tabor 37 Cary 18
2002 Durham Riverside 40 Cary 26
2003 Durham Riverside 38 Cary 30
2004 Durham Riverside 35 Cary 28
2005 Cary 34 Davie County 32

AAA
YEAR CHAMPION RUNNER-UP

1990 T.W. Andrews 51 Kings Mountain 10
1991 T.W. Andrews 38 Central Davidson 13
1992 T.W. Andrews 34 Statesville 27
1993 Sun Valley 50 Northwest Guilford 16

1994 High Point Central 34 West Carteret 29
1995 Winston-Salem Parkland 27 Ragsdale 25
1996 Winston-Salem Parkland 40 Havelock 25
1997 Havelock 48 Winston-Salem Parkland 28
1998 Eden John M. Morehead 32 North Gaston 28
1999 Eden John M. Morehead 40 Waynesville Tuscola 24
2000 Fuquay-Varina 36 Waynesville Tuscola 28
2001 Fuquay-Varina 46 Hickory St. Stephens 11
2002 Eden John M. Morehead 34 Hickory St. Stephens 26
2003 Eden John M. Morehead 31 East Gaston 26
2004 Jamestown Ragsdale 40 Eden John M. Morehead 25
2005 Orange 30 East Gaston 28

A/AA
YEAR CHAMPION RUNNER-UP

1990 Dixon 38 Mitchell County 28
1991 Albemarle 40 Mount Pleasant 23
1992 Dixon 30 Avery County 25
1993 East Davidson 27 Ashe Central 26
1994 Dixon 36 North Henderson 28
1995 East Davidson 28 Mount Pleasant 25
1996 West Henderson 28 East Davidson 26
1997 Alleghany 30 East Davidson 27
1998 North Wilkes 40 East Davidson 32
1999 Alleghany 37 Currituck 36
2000 West Lincoln 36 Southern Vance 23
2001 Canton Pisgah 31 Southern Vance 30

AA
YEAR CHAMPION RUNNER-UP

2002 Southern Vance 36 Canton Pisgah 34
2003 Southern Vance 34 Brevard 30

2004 McMichael 45 West Stokes 16
2005 Bandys 41 Croatan 15

A
YEAR CHAMPION RUNNER-UP

2002 Alleghany 48 South Davidson 18
2003 South Davidson 37 Alleghany 27
2004 Elkin 34 West Davidson 32
2005 Chatham Central 43 East Surry 36

The North Carolina High School Athletic Association, located in Chapel Hill, North Carolina, provided all contents related to the North Carolina High School State Championship Results as a courtesy.

26

Preparing for the State Tournament

A Coliseum view of the North Carolina State Tournament arena with nine mats on the floor.

*A*s a high school senior at West Henderson, I was motivated to find a way to get to the state tournament. The 1979 NCHSAA Sectional qualifying matches would be held at Tuscola High School in Haywood County. After losing in a 15-16 match the year before as a junior at the *sectionals against a kid named Gant from Pisgah High School in Canton, I spent a full year working hard in the weight room and wrestling freestyle matches in an effort to improve my chances of making the trip to Winston Salem as a twelfth grader.*

I had posted a successful season during my senior year and as the seeds were arranged to decide the sectionals brackets I was fairly confident about my chances to compete at the state tournament. I won my early matches in the sectionals and I was very confident about my opponent in the sectional quarterfinals. I had pinned him twice during the regular season. His name was Wes Lyda and he went to Edneyville High School. Edneyville was a I-A small school in Henderson County that has been consolidated into what is now called North Henderson High School. Wes was younger than me and in the matches preceding the sectionals I had been able to make pretty short work of his efforts to compete with my more experienced approach to the game. In fact, because of my prior experience with Wes I had already begun to look ahead to the next possible opponent. And what I saw was a little scary. I knew that if I could just beat Wes I would face an intimidating opponent from Enka High that I had somehow avoided in the duals and tournaments that preceded the sectionals.

It was still the first day of competition when Wes and I took the mat. I quickly shot a double leg takedown. I lifted him high and dropped him toward his back and he fought to his base. Apparently he had brought his "A" game for the sectionals. And in truth I had not brought mine for this match. I was already preparing in mind for Larry Martin that I would see in the semi-finals from Enka. I had looked past this kid from Edneyville. And that would prove to be a mistake. Like an idiot I put in a cross body ride on Wes, and I at that time, had little experience with that particular wrestling strategy. Wes began to flail and I heard my knee pop. It was at that point that I got the leg out and actually did go on to turn him over and pin him in the third period. But the damage had already been done. It was not an injury that kept me from walking, but it was messed up to the point that I was having trouble getting in a good offensive stance.

That night I stayed over at Cliff Wilson's house so that we didn't have to drive all the way back up to my home in Big Willow the next morning before traveling back to the sectional semi-final matches at Tuscola. I began to feel the leg start to stiffen as I tried to sleep at my coach's house. I woke up early and got in a hot bathtub to try and loosen up the knee joint. It seemed to help a little. When we arrived at the gym I began one of the greatest theatrical performances of my life. Although the leg was killing me I attempted to walk around as if nothing had ever happened on that night before.

When we got to the weigh-in room it was full of half clad young men who were qualifying their body weight on the scales for the second day of championship competition. As we stood in line, several of the coaches began to discuss the upcoming semi-final matches, my coach included. My opponent as I mentioned would be Larry Martin. Larry had already pinned all of the quality opponents in the mountains at the 185lb weight class, one of which was Jerome Conley from Brevard who had beaten me in a 6-4 dual match during the regular season. I really could have done without all of the historical commentary that was being disseminated among the coaches as we waited for our turn to weigh in. But it only got worse.

I was short and small for a 185 competitor. I am 5'8" tall and I only weighed about 175lbs. The truth is I probably should have wrestled 167, but I always attempted to keep my weight up in the early season for football. The fact that I was smaller seemed to encourage the discussion about my potential demise as I was preparing to face Larry Martin, combined with the fact that Jim Whitmer always had the Enka kids primed and ready for state competition.

The next thing that came out of a coach's mouth was from the head coach at TC Roberson. He was a very animated man anyway. I believe he actually taught drama at the school. He would often whistle and scream during matches to push his competitors toward a chance to win. But this time he was talking to my coach about me. His kid was a very good wrestler and he had already been pinned by Larry Martin. As the discussion grew, it kind of got out of hand. The TC Coach finally stated, even in front of me, that there was no way that I had a chance to win. My coach Cliff Wilson defended my potential chance at winning. It became so verbally intensive and blatant that the coach from TC Roberson finally said "I'll bet you a steak dinner that he gets beat." And of course Coach Wilson said "fine, we'll see who wins when the semi-finals are over." It wasn't ugly but it was a little intense. I just kept thinking "coach have you forgotten about my knee?"

As we neared the time to go on the mat for this semi-final match that could automatically ensure my chance to make it to the finals of the sectionals and immediately qualify me to go to the regionals and possibly to the state tournament, I have to admit that I was dealing with some doubt, especially with my injury. But I had worked hard for a long time and at this time the sport had begun to equip me with a level of confidence that wavered very little, even under such dire potential consequences. As I warmed up, I did what I could do to loosen the knee joint and I never let on that it even bothered me because I was afraid he would identify it as the weakness that it was.

I was lucky to have the kind of man that Cliff Wilson was in my corner that day. If he had a lack of confidence in my potential to win, he never let it show. As I did on every occasion before a match I said a personal prayer. I asked that both opponents be alright and let thy will be done and the whistle blew. Larry was a big and physical opponent. I first attempted to go head to head in the match tying up with him in a collar tie. He sucked me into his grip like a vacuum cleaner. This was a mistake I would not make again. I narrowly escaped the clutches of his massive vice-grip-like lock that would have surely minimized my chances for success had I continued to attempt to battle him in a head-on scenario. He was surefooted for a big man and his style of play was painfully effective when it was delivered under his terms and conditions. I did not go unscathed from the experience. The extra tooth that protruded under my upper lip due to the fact that I would not run into my first dentist until a later time in my life when I was twenty-one years old, had ripped a hole in my lip that was spewing blood all over him and me. As the action was stopped I began to formulate a plan and a hope for finding a way to survive and somehow overcome this well-skilled and physical beast of an opponent.

As we returned to the action on the mat the hard lesson that I had taken when I tied up with him was well understood. I began to shoot a primitive version of a low single leg takedown on Larry that allowed me to gain some advantage in the match. I know longer attempted to wade into his strength. I was forced to be creative with my approach, to the point of allowing him to escape from my clutches if it meant that I would be limited to wrestling under the conditions that allowed him to use his superior size and overall power. I held on to my lead in the match until the final whistle blew. When the match was finally over I had defeated the Enka opponent by a score of 9 to 4, none of which were awarded for back points. And I certainly looked far worse from the physical experience than did Larry.

The adrenalin had washed away the painful sting of the knee injury and the elation of knowing I had burst through the first gate toward the state tournament minimized the importance of the laceration and the blood in my mouth. All that I had worked for since begging to participate in this game in the ninth grade had come to a level of fruition that would eventually pave the way for college and a career.

On the second day of the state tournament at Parkland High School in Winston Salem, NC, the head coach from TC Roberson took Coach Wilson and I both to the "Western Sizzlin" for a big fat steak. Somewhat thankfully, I never had to wrestle Larry Martin again, either at the regionals or at the state tournament. He did make it to the NCHSAA State Tournament that year in 1979 and from my perspective he certainly deserved to go.

"Bloody." 1979 NCHSAA Sectional Semi-final match, Darrell McDowell, West Henderson vs. Larry Martin-State Qualifier from Enka High School.

There are few things that have the potential to define a young person's level of strength, perseverance, and disciplined commitment that compare to the recognition and rewards that await any individual who has earned the right to declare that he has won a state championship in the sport of wrestling. It is revered as such an important level of status that it becomes as much apart of who they are, as it is a monumental example of what they have been able to accomplish.

In November of each year, it becomes the dream of hundreds of thousands of young people, and their coaches, all over America to clear the path that leads to a state championship. This symbol of excellence is used as the focal point that almost all wrestlers and coaches use to motivate a level of progress and performance throughout each competitive season. These young men and women set their sights on a highly prized, and eternally recognized way of leaving their mark on the history of the game, in an effort to forge a permanently engraved element of athletic excellence in their schools and communities, that will be highlighted by the athletic associations in their home states.

Each state has its own process and schedule for determining how these standouts will be selected and where the events will take place. But this ideal, and the vision that begins to evolve with each year's march toward becoming a state champion is clearly defined by the purity of the process that was mentioned in the earlier pages of this book. Each wrestler will begin to decide his/her own destiny as he fights through the seeded and bracketed sectional, and/or regional tournaments that are designed to sort out who will have the right to compete at the state level. As teams are constructed throughout each year, the details and strategies that include the development of schedules and the arrangement of practice sessions are ultimately affected and influenced by the preparation for the state tournament.

The desire to cut through the extreme levels of competition, minimize injury, and improve performance, are contoured to ensure successful participation in this final and most important state championship tournament. Not only coaches, but individual competitors, will be continuously mindful of arranging their goals with consideration for how each one will enhance their chances of standing on the highest podium when the gold medal is hung around the neck of the state champion.

There was a time when only one state champion was designated across all classifications with regard to school sizes for each of the states in America. I often hear the comment made that "that was when men were men." I guess that is an arguable conclusion when compared with many state tournaments that now recognize more than one state champion.

Most states now use a format in which the various classifications are broken down based on school size. Each division awards medals for place winners in each weight category. Though some would say that the level of competition has been watered down because of the escalation in the number of champions named, others, myself included, welcome the chance to see the sport grow because of the improved access to the potential rewards and successes that are now available for an increased number of participants in the sport. Much of this movement was initiated in North Carolina by the inspired efforts of people like Mike Raybon at Ragsdale High School who felt that the divided format was in the best interest of the most athletes.

Leaders and coaches in small high schools will now be able to compete in a classification that will allow for the smaller schools to have a reasonable chance to succeed. This should help encourage their investment in purchasing mats and uniforms, and for some, adding new wrestling programs that would have never been considered as a necessary component of their school, prior to the changes in the alignment process. School administrators and athletic directors will no longer have the ready-made excuse or obstacle of past struggles or failures to compete with larger schools.

There is one distinct advantage for students with the more recent way of naming state champions. The level of success among participants breeds an enthusiastic base of competitors that reap what is perceived to be the ultimate bounty in the sport. It is no secret that there are many small school state champions that participate at the A and AA categories of competition that will have abilities that supersede the performance levels of individuals at their same weight class in the larger AAA, or even AAAA divisions of the athletic alignments. But, the smaller schools will not have the overall potential to draw from as large a pool of athletes in their building as would the coaches from the larger schools.

This dynamic makes for interesting non-conference and out of state match-ups in the early part of the season when schools often compete in cross category tournaments and matches. Quite often, because of the clear opportunities that exist in wrestling for coaches who are attentive to creativity, discipline and detail, and for wrestlers who welcome the challenge of competing against what appear to be unequal odds, the "David and Goliath" situation can become a reality. This scenario creates substantial highs and lows among teams and individual competitors, and offers exciting opportunities for fans. These invitational tournaments are often planned and contoured to ensure strong competition among the teams, while testing individual wrestlers to a significant level of reflection about what they will need to do to improve their performance as they prepare to compete in their own classification at the state championship tournament.

27

Dissolving the Mystique

A Ragsdale athlete on the Podium, winning the Gold Medal at the NCHSAA Wrestling State Tournament Championships.

*W*hen I took over what was at the time an ailing West Henderson program in the fall of 1986 there was a variety of issues to consider. One particular situation was the quality of the personnel that was already there. Brian

Cartee was a 125 pound kid that was a senior. Everything he and the others on the team were saying about his past performance indicated that he had always done well during the regular season, but he had never been able to get out of the regional tournament to even qualify for the state tournament.

After watching his performance in the early practices, it was clear that he was a very talented individual. He was a great kid with a big smile and a neat personality. But it appeared that what he really needed was a sustained opportunity to build some confidence and a chance to enter the regional tournament with a sense of personal courage that would allow him to believe he deserved to get to the state tournament because of his hard work. He needed some battle scars to prove it.

When I was finished with the next four months of his life, he would have no doubt about where he stood as a competitor in North Carolina high school wrestling.

When I developed the schedule for the year I had at least doubled the level of competitive matches and tournaments that Brian and the other kids were accustomed to facing. That year Rex Wells was the head coach at Brevard High School. He had the best team in the mountains at that time. They were in our conference and they were only about twenty miles down the road from the West Henderson campus. I took full advantage of that opportunity. Also at Brevard was a young man by the name of Timmy Ellenberger. He had been a state champion as a sophomore, and had finished third his junior year and was heavily favored to win the state tournament again as a senior. And he just happened to be at Brian Cartee's weight class.

Brian did not lack the desire to be a champion. He did need to improve his skills, his work ethic, and he needed the opportunity to employ his craft in a competitive environment. By the time we were finished with the season that year he had been immersed in all he could stand of all those circumstances. It seemed that almost every tournament I had scheduled along with the conference dual match, conference tournament, regional tournament and state tournament all included a chance for Brian to wrestle the state champion from Brevard. And we never missed the opportunity or dodged the chance to face him.

This made for a long hard road for Brian. But any of the mysteries that he had about the quality of his performance were cleared up during the battles he had with such a quality opponent as Timmy. And facing the Brevard team along with Enka that year on so many occasions had the same sobering yet empowering effect on our young program at West Henderson.

When they called out the names of the wrestlers that would compete for the final match in the state down at Chapel Hill that year at the 125 pound weight class, as expected Timmy Ellenberger stood on one side of the mat. But no one would have predicted that his opponent would have been the young man from West Henderson who had not even been able to get out of the regional tournament in the years past. Yes, Brian had made it all the way to the finals of the state tournament that first year that I returned to my alma mater at West. And his reward for his hard work and dedication was one last shot at the young man that in my mind will always be the reason that we were able to make such tremendous progress with Brian's efforts that year.

Brian won every tournament and every match that year that did not include Timmy. But, the level of performance that he aspired to in his effort to compete with the state champion brought tremendous growth and a variety of rewards to Brian's personal success. Brian's eventual record was 31 and 7 that year and each and every one of his losses were to Timmy Ellenberger. We had a choice about changing his weight class that year but chose to take one last shot at the Brevard Champion. Brian went on to lose the match to Timmy in the finals of the state tournament in a hard fought battle and finished as the runner-up in that spring of 1987.

But, he and I both believe to this day that those early battles that were fought during the season ensured his ability to get to the finals. He had a dogfight in the semi-finals with Mark Horn that he won by a single point. Mark was a very capable and well respected opponent from Trinity High School near High Point that Brian defeated to get to the finals. The example Brian set and the drama that accompanied the effort he made to get to the state finals that year helped set the stage for five more West Henderson wrestlers to eventually win their matches in the state finals during my coaching career at the school And one of the five champions pinned all of his opponents before the end of the second period in each match of the state tournament in 1989. That young man just happened to be Brandon Cartee, Brian's brother.

Brian's efforts during that year dissolved many of the myths about his ability to compete at the state level of competition and helped inspire many others to begin prescribing their own vision for finding success in the program.

As you begin to prepare athletes for this ultimate competition in Scholastic Amateur Wrestling, be aware of the dynamic that will naturally exist when wrestlers head toward the regional qualifying and state tournament competition. We often spend a great deal of time as coaches reinforcing the significance of what it would it mean for a young man to become a state champion. Do not lose sight of the fact that when you assume the responsibility to push these young people to exceptional levels of competition, you will be dealing with all of the hormones, insecurities and vulnerabilities of 15, 16, and 17 year-old students. But with hard work and personal commitment, some of them might dare to buy into your dream. And some may surpass your expectations.

We often spend all season making this venture into an almost surreal expedition of opportunity and fantasy to motivate these young people to compete in this one exceptional event. Be very careful about how you prepare these young men to put their plans into practice when you actually arrive at this prestigious tournament.

All competitors will handle the psychological and emotional aspects of this opportunity in their own personal way. But for some of them, once they arrive at the tournament, they have to be reminded not to freak out. Clarify the reality of the situation for them. Infuse them with the stabilizing truth that it is just another tournament. Most skilled and passionate competitors will not be affected by this potential "deer in the headlights" look that overcomes some athletes during their first time in the state tournament arena. But your athletes need to be made aware of the potential for an unnecessary mental or emotional meltdown prior to their arrival at the coliseum for the first day of state competition. Identify and destroy this hypersensitive possibility long before the beginning of the ceremonies and celebrations.

This is a time when you will often see individuals begin to call on their faith in themselves and their confidence about their level of preparation. Many begin to draw on their faith in God to help them diffuse some of the thoughts of inadequacy that can paralyze a first-time competitor. Just make sure that you have prepared them throughout the year and be prepared to help them through a moment of insecurity it if happens at the site. Your prescription for addressing the issue, if it comes up, will be different for each competitor. You will know them well enough, by that point in the season, that you will likely be able to infuse them with a well-tailored boost of confidence-building commentary. Do not ignore the situation. Address it.

Robb Atkinson, West Henderson High School, NC State Champion 1989. Coach Darrell McDowell.

For these first-timers, the most difficult challenges can be facing their own vulnerabilities and mortalities as they attempt to gather the courage they will need to compete in the matches that lie ahead. If you have done a good job with planning, scheduling, and coaching these young men, most of them will be prepared.

Wrestlers attending the state tournament who have had the benefit of a strong program and have been intensely prepared will normally show up on the mat with a level of confidence that will carry them through the trials that will emerge in the state-wide competition. This is also the time when many will turn to their religion and their faith in God to search for additional ways to help them find balance, and to relieve themselves of any fears or doubts about there performance and their purpose.

Brandon Cartee, West Henderson High School, NC State Champion, 1989. Coach Darrell McDowell.

In fact, at the other end of the scale are a small number of individuals who will flourish in this environment. They will contend at a level well beyond all expectations, superseding past performances to a level of execution that has not been experienced at any other time in their wrestling careers. An undefeated record does not always ensure great success at the state tournament, nor does a less than perfect regular season record condemn a competitor to failure in this most prestigious event.

This competition can sometimes produce a unique set of circumstances surrounding the ultimate levels of successful participation by its qualifiers. Individuals are often faced with a sense of urgency and expectation that is self-imposed to a degree that can dramatically affect their long-held ambition about becoming a state champion. This tournament can have a positive, or a negative, impact on their vision for success.

Rob Heaton, in the white shorts, West Henderson High School, 2x NC State Champion 1992 and 1993. Coach Darrell McDowell.

At this level of competition, injuries, sickness, or a late weigh-in, as strange and as impossible as that sounds, can derail the predicted results of the seeded brackets that are used to pit individuals against their first round opponents. And, a variety of issues can unseat the expected flow of potential winners throughout the competitive process. A refusal by the athletes to be affected by any possible interruption, or to be affected by the exceptional attributes of their opponents, is in some way at the very exciting and impressive essence of the sport.

The purity of the process that has been discussed throughout this book begins to infuse itself into the hopes and the performances of every wrestler in the building. No competitor in the state tournament can escape the one-on-one realities that display themselves as they begin to step on the mat, under this microscope of expert and unavoidable criticism, alongside extreme possibilities for excessive glory. Each wrestler's every move will be highlighted in front of the largest and most educated group of fans, coaches, and wrestling enthusiasts that most will ever be privileged to endure or enjoy.

As the competition continues, the drama begins to build and the contest begins to develop its own form. Upsets and early pins stir the emotional climate in the auditorium and these warriors begin to reveal their individual attempts to move ever closer to the championship finals. To lose one match is to eliminate what has been a dream for sometimes four years, or for some, a lifetime of dedication and commitment.

As these wrestlers are eliminated from the championship rounds there is also great drama in watching their efforts to pick themselves up and aspire to a new goal of aiming for the next highest possible bronze medal. This becomes the longest road in the tournament, as they begin to wrestle their way back through the consolation bracket, facing other opponents defeated in the early rounds, in a final attempt to stand in a respected place on the podium behind a chance missed to be number one. In some formats, to lose two matches eliminates any chance to get a medal at this event. Many times this enduring process of taking the long hard way toward the medal round provides a glowing indication of real and persevering heroism by individuals who refuse to leave the arena empty-handed.

As the competition begins to thin out the lesser competitors, you will normally begin to see fewer pins and less decisive wins begin to emerge on the mats. Even the consolation rounds become dogfights for survival.

After the first day of competition there are lots of decisions being made by the various competitors. Some are gaining steam and some appear to be cutting their losses. Some will even begin to say, "Well at least I made it to state," and others will admit "Well tomorrow is going to be tough," and a few will dare say, "This is my time to prove that I will be the state champion." And the results and the memories of their accomplishments will begin to vary and differ as they begin to live out their circumstances. Some will make excuses, and for others their exceptional goals will have been justly confirmed. The reality that there will only be one winner in each weight class in this sport is never clearer than in the heat of the battles that evolve in this prestigious contest of wills.

There are other issues that can factor into this roller coaster of adrenalin and competition as they prepare for the second day of the tournament. Some of the individuals will have rarely stayed away from home on overnight trips, as basic as that sounds. And they may not sleep a wink during the night before what will be, for some of them, the semifinals of the state tournament. All that they have worked for in the sport of wrestling will be decided in the results of one next match. Six minutes of heated competition will lie between them and the opportunity to stand in front of thousands of screaming fans with at least a silver medal, and an opportunity to contend for the greatest treasure in this scholastic sport, and a chance to compete for the gold medal in the most pivotal contest of their lives.

Kyle Kuykendall,West Henderson, NC State Champion 1990 coached by Darrell McDowell.

I would like to suggest that to the untrained eye an outstanding match could be confused and viewed by the least educated individuals in the audience as a boring performance. These folks clearly have no way to appreciate the exceptional level of talent and perseverance it takes to combat an equally matched opponent, in such a vigilant and ambitious event as the championship rounds of the state tournament. Fans often want to see opponents crushed under a dominating, or lopsided level of competition, that can actually happen quite often, in other less competitive arenas of wrestling events.

But, at the state tournament, the competition is often stiff and consistent. And, for the rest of us, unlike the less experienced fans, we marvel and relate to the intensity. We understand the undying effort, and the persistent will to pursue what is such an exceptional dream. Pins do sometimes happen, even in the finals of the championship matches, and it is exciting when it does occur. But the artistic excellence of the sport can often be found in the skillful execution of a successful game plan by each opponent, and in the strategic efforts of each competitor to disarm, and disrupt, the mental, emotional, and athletic efforts of what stands in the way of state championship goals.

For the educated fan the drama that is found in the championship semi-final round compares easily with the intensity found in the championship finals, because in this intensive round, all four competitors have already pictured themselves as potential champions with a reasonable sense of hope and confidence about reaching their dreams. And most can already taste what it would be like to make the trip to the next match in the celebrated final round of the state tournament.

28

The Finals

Trey Curtain, High Point Andrews, attempts to defend his NCHSAA State Title. Coach Wally Burke.

In North Carolina, the High School Athletic Association sponsors the Individual State Wrestling Championship Tournament. The NCHSAA sites have been moved and adjusted over the years to include arenas that have ranged and varied from locations in Winston Salem, Chapel Hill,

Charlotte, and Greensboro, North Carolina. The most recent site has found a way back to a once favored town for hosting the event in Winston Salem, North Carolina.

The NCHSAA has provided much flexibility over the years with the on-going development of the procedures, site determination, and the overall parameters for coordinating the State Tournament. The format has changed with the addition of the crowning of Annual Dual Team State Champions, segmenting the varying classifications with separate and distinct individual tournaments, and hosting all Individual Championships at one simultaneous event. These were major innovations that included a great deal of collaboration between league officials and North Carolina coaches.

Dick Knox

One individual that used a gentlemen's approach to presiding over the event for many years and worked closely with all coaches in the state of North Carolina as the Deputy Executive Director of the NCHSAA was Mr. Dick Knox. Dick was straight forward with his communication and appeared open to any ideas that would keep us between the legal and sportsmanlike boundaries of the game and would move us forward to improve the maturity of each event. Dick has recently retired from his position with the NCHSAA as a League Official in Chapel Hill, North Carolina, and a new cast of well-qualified administrators have carried on where he left off. But his many years of dedication have had an effective impact on the growth and the success of wrestling in the high schools of North Carolina.

Dick Knox, Deputy Executive Director, NCHSAA.

Que Tucker, another outstanding and experienced representative for the NCHSAA, will now assume the wrestling responsibilities that Dick so effectively administered during his long and distinguished career.

The state tournament was held at Parkland High School during the 1970's and has since outgrown that venue. It is now held at the Lawrence Joel Veteran's Memorial Coliseum near the campus of Wake Forest University. This geographically centralized location and appropriate arena size appears to be well-suited for hosting this outstanding event. The tournament officials are residents of the area, and the level of communication and organization has been very effective and efficient during recent years.

It takes a monumental effort to make the state tournament a successful event. And it takes hundreds of organizers and volunteers to make it work. One particular individual that has been able to make the kinds of contributions that have changed the complexion of the state tournament over a period of many years has been Mike Raybon. Mike was the State Individual Tournament Director in North Carolina for many years. He along with Kathy Dick have spent much time and energy over the years, organizing and administrating the intensive efforts it has taken to make this tournament such a great success.

Coach Raybon' current responsibilities with the Tournament now include his participation as an active consultant to the NCHSAA's State Wrestling Tournament's current director, Mr. Lee Hebbard. Lee is from Eastern Guilford High School in Gibsonville, North Carolina, also in the Greensboro area. He appears to be doing an outstanding job with directing the event.

Mike Raybon

Mike Raybon is as much a part of North Carolina wrestling and the NCHSAA's State Wrestling Championship's as any other traditional part of the process. He is a former coach at Ragsdale High School, where he commandeered the Ragsdale Tigers to three NC High School State Tournament Championships as Head Wrestling Coach and Assistant Principal. He is now Athletic Director at the same school, located in the Greensboro area of North Carolina.

Mike Raybon, Former Head Wrestling Coach at Ragsdale High School and Former NCHSAA State Tournament Director. Works closely as a consultant with the current Tournament Director.

Coach Raybon's intensive and sometimes crusty approach to moving the tournament forward appears to have encouraged many improvements in the operation of the process. He has an ambitious and visionary plan for ensuring the on-going success of the state tournament that mimics the disciplined efforts he used to accomplish the impressive victories he enjoyed as an outstanding high school wrestling coach for many years at Ragsdale High.

Under his watchful eye and guidance, the state competition has become a much more progressive and successful event, providing a wide variety of new and exciting opportunities to an increasing number of wrestling competitors in the state. With Coach Raybon's historical perspective, and Mr. Hebbard's effective approach to initiating the operation of the event, it appears that together they have created effective procedures for directing the tournament in a framework that considers the essential needs of the competitors, understands the ambitions of the coaches, and appreciates the important details that ensure a legitimate and exciting experience for all who attend and participate in the process.

The future of this event appears to be brighter than ever, and it couldn't be in better hands as Coach Raybon continues to generate opportunities for the young people associated with this sport. As a former Appalachian State wrestler, forty-two years ago, he is one of the pillars of consistency that continue to perpetuate the culture and the fraternal order of wrestling in North Carolina, and in this part of the country.

Coach Raybon is also the current North Carolina "Athletic Director of the Year" in the state of North Carolina, and he along with Kathy Dick also recently received the honor of being inducted into the National Wrestling Hall of Fame in Stillwater, Oklahoma for their contributions to the sport of wrestling and for the monumental work they have done with improving the state tournament structure in North Carolina.

Officials
Joe Jones and Bill Wheeler

Another area of importance that sets the pace and dictates the success of the state tournament is the quality of the officials at the event. These very necessary components of the process are sometimes unfairly designated and identified as the part of the process that some people love to hate. Their judgments and decisions can become a quick excuse for any shortfall that occurs in an individual wrestler's expected level of performance. The referees that are selected to officiate in the prestigious state tournament are normally selected because of their consistent and continued level of success in the game. As each of the referees is named and recognized before the final matches ensue, many of the faces of these men in striped shirts have become easily recognizable, due to their longevity and valued participation in this event.

Joe Jones has been a highly recognizable wrestling official for over fifty years.

There are several referees who have established themselves as stabilizing and perennial fixtures with the officiating crew. The attendance and participation of Joe Jones and Bill Wheeler have become a regular occurrence. They are two well-tenured officials who have whistled the start and finish of high school matches and tournaments since I was a high school competitor in the old days. Both were refereeing matches at the North Carolina State Tournament that I participated in as a scholastic wrestler when it was held at the Parkland High School site in Winston Salem, North Carolina in 1979. Their lengthy relationship with the state tournament helps to prove the depth and the reliability of the structure, and the level of commitment that is bred into this valuable and exceptional arena of sport.

Bill Wheeler has been officiating wrestling for nearly thirty years.

As I look around the state tournament facility each year, there is a visible thread of understanding and connectivity that surrounds this wrestling event. It has clearly become a part of our lives that we not only enjoy, but have a need and a desire to be associated with as a part of who we are and what we represent, that is verified in our annual return to the competition.

29

The Heart of the Journey

As the arena begins to fill with spectators on the Saturday evening of the NCHSAA Individual State Tournament, the crowds of people quickly begin negotiating for position as they attempt to acquire the best seats in house. The electricity in the air begins to build as the final mats are moved to the center of the facility to their championship positions. The orchestration of this event is normally a smooth articulation of complex logistics that begin to happen like clockwork.

When the consolation rounds have ended, those mats are broken down and removed from the building to help create the space that will be needed for what has evolved as an important tradition in the North Carolina State Championships that is known as the "Parade of Champions." All wrestlers that will be competing for the gold medals and the others that have been successful in competing for lesser medals will be recognized for their efforts in a formal celebration of their victories, at that escalating point in the tournament. These young men are hailed and rewarded by a display of appreciation and a multi-faceted array of spotlights and music, in a parade of recognition that occurs just before the final round begins. At this point in the tournament, if you look around the arena, you will begin to see the depth and degree of what is meant by the fraternal order that is created in the amateur wrestling world. The clear and visible expression of what has been described and discussed with regard to identifying the characteristics associated with building a wrestling culture start to evidence themselves in the ambiance and the atmosphere of the championship arena.

As you near the progression of the events leading up to these championship finals, you will begin to see a wide variety of descriptive circumstances that illustrate how important this event has become to so many people. You can almost pick the former competitors and coaches out of the crowd by their physical posture, the way they carry themselves, and their almost visible sense of understanding of what is about to occur on the floor of the arena. As the stands begin to fill with parents, coaches, college scouts, and wrestlers who didn't make the final round of competition, there is a general atmosphere of excitement and anticipation. In the population of this audience, there are very few individuals who won't be able to appreciate what is at stake for these final championship competitors.

This final event in the tournament has become a mecca for former coaches, wrestlers, parents and fans that have all, in some way, found themselves to be members of this pilgrimage. They come to this place to fill a need that is associated with a desire to be in close proximity to this life-changing event, in a climate that allows for dreams to be fulfilled. Most of them have their own stories that relate to their own experiences in a similar arena, at a different time or place, in their own lives. These spectators attend this final event expecting to be infused with a wide array of emotions before they exit the arena. They anticipate, and welcome, the unpredictable feelings of excitement, pride, fear, compassion, surprise, frustration, controversy, and even a sense of envy for some, about a vicarious chance to relive what will take place on the mat in the drama of these final championship matches.

As the lights begin to dim, and the balloons around the entrance of the arena floor begin to shake with the rustle of activity, the excitement about what is to come begins to reveal itself. Separated by divisions and weight classes, in a uniform yet individualized display of excited anticipation and pride, the "Parade of Champions" begins to unfold. As the athletes are ushered into the arena by the powerful musical sounds of Queen's "We are the Champions," the glare of the spotlights adds even greater attention and energy to the escalation of emotions that are generated on the floor of the building and reverberated to every empty seat in the house as each row of spectators come to their feet to greet, praise and cheer their favorite wrestlers on to victory.

Parade of Champions at the NCHSAA State Tournament.

The Heart of the Journey

It is at this point that, if you ever had a doubt about the importance of the struggle it takes to get to the state tournament, all of your questions are answered. When the national anthem is sung by a local student or a special guest, and the hair begins to stand up on the back of your neck, or your stomach begins to churn with nervous energy, your emotions will be moved even further with a final anticipation of the competition.

As the lights come on again, the frenzy of warm-up routines is played out with fever and intensity as each competitor attempts to rid themselves of their final fears and anxieties. The final pre-game drama is ignited as the announcer asks this superior accumulation of potential champions to "clear the mats" and the 103-pound wrestlers start the action. Any number of possible dramas begins to unveil after the first whistle blows. And all the hopes and prayers, and the extreme efforts that have occurred on their way to this exceptional level of performance, are culminated in the six-minute matches that follow.

The crowds soak up the action as they attempt to will their favorites a way to win. As the tournament proceeds new champions are crowned and some old champions are dethroned, making the way for any variety of life-changing opportunities to erupt out of this experience. Tears of joy, frustration, and despair are commonplace among any number of stakeholders in the arena. Competitors, parents, and coaches respond to their own fates with extreme levels of elation, disappointment and varying degrees of disciplined composure as the individual realities of the wrestlers are decided by the final whistle in each championship match. Their ultimate levels of success and their historical position of recognition are defined in a very public and well-recorded fashion.

Trey Curtain, High Point Andrews High School, 2x NC State Champion following his victory in the final match. Coach Wally Burke.

When it is all said and done and the medals are handed out, the pictures are taken, and the brackets are given to the champions, a mood of closure, success, and a humble acceptance of the new realities, begin to release the enormous pressures that have been building for four months of physical, mental, and emotional engagement. It is finally decided in a festive celebration of discipline and manhood, in a kind of competition that is so elite, that in reality, though there are many disappointments, there are no real losers.

The real rewards for participating at this level of competition in the wrestling game will continue to be reaped for the rest of their lives. The relationships that are forged, the work ethic that has been learned, the efforts to survive failure, and the opportunities to manage success will be continuously available for the taking. Each wrestler will have equipped himself at a level of usefulness and expertise in the areas of discipline, leadership and work ethic that will always be a part of what they do, and who they are. When conversations erupt about what has been accomplished in their lives, whether they've won or lost in the state wrestling tournament, this competitive experience will fall somewhere on their list of credits, and probably somewhere near the top.

The lessons learned from participating in this game will trickle into their confidence and inspire their ambition in almost everything they do. The pride in their efforts, the love of their sport, their faith in themselves, and the courage to proceed will serve them well, as they endure the challenges and celebrate the successes that will await each one of them as they pursue the rest of their lives and their dreams.

Cary High School Wrestlers celebrating one of their numerous championship victories after being crowned NCHSAA State Champions. Coach-Jerry Winterton. Photo provided by David Maney II, CHS Sports Information Director.

Epilogue

I have always had a compelling need to make some kind of contribution back to the sport that has changed my life for the better. In wrestling it takes a series of processes to come to a point on the mat when you are effectively prepared to face a challenge. The process of writing this book has been filled with many parallels that compare closely to what I have tried to accomplish with the young men I've worked with on the mat.

This effort has required a level of diligence and an open mind about receiving advice that mirrors the demands I expected from my athletes. Thankfully, the people that I have worked with during this process have used the same level of consideration and care that I aspired to use with my wrestlers.

I owe a great deal to the efforts of Casey Hurley, Al Proffit and Gayle Moller at Western Carolina University for immersing me in a challenging level of academic tasks in the Doctoral Program. Their encouragement and level of expectation with the coursework helped give me a solid academic foundation and the confidence to pursue this effort.

Another parallel that played itself out in the development of the book was in the level of personal risk taking that was necessary to describe many of the realities that were exposed in the text. I owe a great deal to Tom and Francine

Costello at Word Association Publishers for their frank critiques of the writing and their steadfast and patient approach to ensuring a level of success with my efforts to express what I had such a dire need to reveal about the importance of this game.

Biography

Darrell McDowell

Darrell McDowell is a school administrator in the Henderson County Public School System in North Carolina. In his twenty years in education, he has taught Physical Education and In-School Suspension and he has coached wrestling, football, and track. McDowell began wrestling as a student at Rugby Junior and West Henderson High Schools and continued when he attended Pembroke State and Appalachian State Universities. He is currently working on his Doctoral Degree in Educational Leadership at Western Carolina University in Cullowhee. Darrell and his wife make their home in Hendersonville, North Carolina with their three children, Candice, Cameron and Christin.